HOW TO TEACH YOUR CHILD PIANO

Even If You Can't Play Yourself!

LEVEL 2

By Stephanie Parker

Table of Contents

Introduction:

There is a false idea that in order for your child to learn to play piano you must pay hundreds of dollars each month for private instruction and piano materials. Granted, once a student reaches a certain level of achievement, then a private instructor would be necessary to continue their progress. However, **the early levels of piano can certainly be taught by any involved parent**. You do not have to have years of private lessons to do this. You do not even have to have had one private lesson to do this.

This book will make it easy to understand what your child needs to know and how to help them. YOU are your child's piano teacher. Not only are you saving literally hundreds of dollars every month, but the time you will get as you teach your child piano will build special memories that will last a lifetime.This is meant to be learned with a parent overseeing their practice to make sure they are following the techniques presented.

This book can be used from kindergarten through adulthood. The pacing will vary based on your child's age. It is recommended to not work faster than 1 lesson per week for K-5th grade. It is recommended not to work faster than 2 lessons per week for 5th grade through 9th grade. 10th grade on, it is possible to do 3 lessons a week. Once the material becomes challenging for your child to master, slow down to 1 lesson a week no matter what their age. The goal is to make this book copy in person lessons as much as possible. Set a specific day and time each week to give your child a lesson.

At each weeks lesson, your child should demonstrate, without help, the previous week lessons practice log items. If they are unable to do so, then repeat the previous weeks lesson. Repeat lessons as many times as necessary until there is a mastery of the subject material.

This book will work best when paired with the supplement theory book for this volume. The more hands on practice and repetition your child does, the easier the skills will become.Do not start this book unless your child has mastered the skills in the first book.

Starting each lesson - teach all the new concepts in each lesson. Before you begin teaching the next weeks lesson, you should hear all their homework from their practice log including the practice song. If any of their homework is challenging for them, that lesson should be repeated instead of moving on.

You will see something call "Parent Answer" after new songs that your child is learning. This is for the parents reference only. It is an aide to help assure you that your child is playing the song they are learning correctly. DO NOT let your child see this answer at any point in them learning the song. Children who learn piano by having the notes written in for them are not truly learning piano. Those kids end up not being able to progress beyond a certain point and become frustrated and often quit piano. If you find an in person teacher who regularly writes in most or all of the notes to your child's song....RUN!

This book is dedicated to my son, David, who taught me how to be a teacher with our many hours of homeschooling. Also, thank you to my amazing husband who put in countless hours editing and teaching me how to format this book. You are the only reason this book was possible. I'd be lost without you, honey!

CHAPTER 1: Playing in Locations Not at C Position

LESSON 1

BEGINNING THIS BOOK

Before you begin this book please make sure your child has mastered all the skills in the previous book. Piano is a cumulative skill like math. If you move on before they have mastered the foundational skills that came previously, your child will become frustrated, overwhelmed and burn out of piano. Below is a list of the skills your child should be comfortable with. If there are any of these skills your child is unfamiliar with, take some time to make them comfortable with that skill before beginning this book.

Level 1 skills your child should know:

- ❋ C Scale played hands together
- ❋ All bass clef and treble clef note flashcards combined in random order
- ❋ C position (RH on middle C, LH on the C below that)
- ❋ Finger numbers
- ❋ Knowing the notes on the piano (with absolutely NO use of writing the letters on the piano itself)
- ❋ Term flashcards: repeat, half note, quarter note, piano, forte, treble clef, bass clef, sharp, flat, quarter rest, grand staff, staff, dotted half note, whole note, bar line, measure, slur, tie, double bar line, 4/4, 3/4

FLASHCARDS

You will continue to quiz your child daily on the term flashcards we used in the previous level book. We will gradually add to those flashcards several new terms. Make sure you continue to review all the old flashcards as well as any new ones we add throughout this entire book.

We will learn some of the flashcard terms far before we learn to really apply it to music. This is so your child is very familiar with the concept before then having to apply it to a song. This will give them a stronger understanding of the term.

MEZZO PIANO

The first term we will add to our flashcards is mezzo piano. Your child has already learned mezzo forte, so the term mezzo piano should be relatively simple to explain to your child. Just like mf, the term mezzo means medium or moderately (pronounced met - zoh). Piano is a term your child already learned meaning to play softly.

Combining the two terms we get the term mezzo piano or medium/moderately soft. On the front of the flashcard draw the image to the right. On the back write mezzo piano - play medium soft (if your child is older write moderately soft, but I find that younger children struggle with the word moderately and in that case it is fine to teach them medium soft until their vocabulary increases).

mp

PLAYING IN LOCATIONS NOT AT C POSITION

In the last level book, every single song was played at C position. This meant every single song had the right hand starting with the 1 finger on middle C and the left hand with the 5 finger on the C below middle C (Bass C).

We are going to be teaching your child that songs can start anywhere on the piano now. We will be redoing in this chapter several concepts your child has already learned in the previous level. However, we will be applying those concepts now playing at locations other than at the C position which will make it trickier.

NOTE FLASHCARDS

In the previous lesson, when your child practiced their note flashcards they simply had to say the correct note name out loud. Now that they are having to play in locations other than C position it is time to add another element to their flashcard practice.

They should be practicing their flashcards everyday. During this practice time, take a section of the cards and have them identify on the piano the correct location for that note. Over the course of the next year (the entire book), increase the amount of flashcards your child finds the location on the piano for as it becomes easier for them until they can do all the notes.

It might be helpful to print out the image below for you as a guide to make sure they are choosing the correct location.

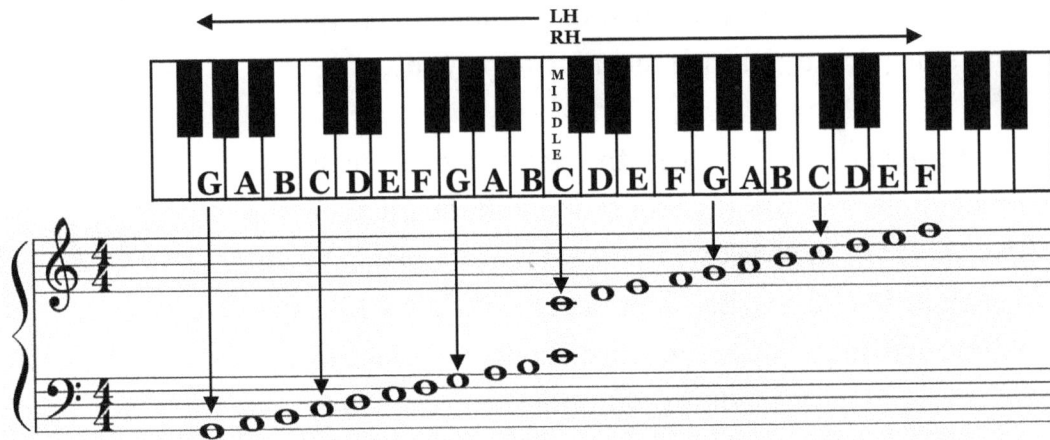

PRACTICE TIME

In the previous level, your child should have achieved a weekly practice time of 4-6 days a week at 10-15 minutes per day. Now that they have reached the next level, the music and concepts are getting increasingly difficult. The daily practice time should increase as a result. If the practice time does not increase, you run the risk of your child becoming frustrated with the weekly lessons.

For this entire level make the weekly practice consist of 4-6 days per week at 15-20 minutes per day practicing.

I encourage you to make this schedule a huge priority in your child's practice. Child who rarely practice and just come to lessons do not progress at a good rate and often end up quitting.

Maybe you know that one week you will only have 2 available days to practice. In that case, double up on those 2 days. Have your child sit down at the piano 2 separate times for 15 minutes each time (30 minutes straight of practice at this level can be too overwhelming for most kids) so they can get in their 4 days of practice.

We all have off weeks or extra busy weeks. When that happens, make sure your child "makes up" the lost time. A week off of practice without making up the lost time should be a rare exception.

TEACHING THE PRACTICE SONG:

The LH is in C position with the 1 finger playing G.

The right hand has moved off of C position. First, ask your child is what note they see in the right hand. They should be able to identify that it is a D from every good boy **D**eserves fudge.

Now ask your child where is that D located. Review with your child the 3 C's: Bass C, middle C, Treble C. Have them play the 3 C's as you call out bass Middle or treble. Then, hold out the 3 flashcards (bass, middle and treble) and have them play the correct C based on the flashcard.

Ask your child if the D in the music is closer to middle C or treble C. Point out that the D in the song is right above treble C. Therefore, they should be playing the D that is 2 D's above middle C.

Now that they have found the correct note, then they need to focus on the finger number that belongs on that note. Make sure they have the 5 finger on treble D. Now that their hands are in place, they don't have to move again for the whole song.

This is the process they should follow for each song in the whole book for finding where to place their hands at the start of the song.

Remember the steps of practice a song. First have them write in the counts and clap the rhythm before attempting to play the notes.

Point out the rest in the RH that occurs on beat 1. Also notice that in the LH on beat 1 the LH plays and holds.

Daily Practice Log (4-6 days @ 15-20 minutes each day):
- ✸ *Flashcards for terms*
- ✸ *Flashcards for all notes (find the location on the piano for some of them)*
- ✸ *Practice song*
- ✸ *Corresponding Theory Chapter*
- ✸ *Hands together C Scale going up and down*
- ✸ *Identify bass, middle, treble C and D*

Stephanie Parker

STEPPING STONES

STEPPING STONES

Practice song answer for parents... Don't let your child see this answer at any time

LESSON 2

Start each lesson by going over each item in the previous weeks practice log. Repeat last weeks lesson if your child cannot complete their practice log independently including playing their homework practice song with approximately 85% accuracy. Do this at the beginning of each lesson the entire level.

WHOLE REST

The next term we will add to our flashcards is whole rest. You taught your child about the quarter rest which received 1 beat of rest/silence. This is the same concept except it gets 4 beats of silence instead of 1.

A whole rest is very similar to a whole note. Both gets 4 beats. A whole note gets 4 beats holding down the note on the piano. A whole rest gets 4 beats of silence. This is called a whole rest and it gets 4 beats of silence.

On the front of the flashcard draw the image above. On the back write whole rest - 4 beats of silence.

There is a trick to remember a whole rest. Teach your child to imagine they are walking along that line and then fall into that big black "hole." Let that remind you that it is a "whole" rest.

The individual symbol is like the image above. However, as shown in the image to the right, when the whole rest is placed in music the top line blends into the staff. You could draw this image on the flashcard as well so they can recognize the whole rest by itself as well as in the staff.

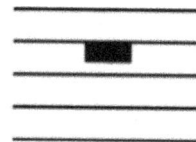

DAMPER PEDAL

Under your piano you will see 3 pedals. If you are using a keyboard you may see only 2 pedals. On either the piano or the keyboard, the damper pedal is the pedal all the way to the right.

Make sure your child only uses their right foot when playing the damper pedal.

This is where you as the instructor becomes

This is a pedal mark. When you see this it means to push the right pedal down.

very important. There is a specific way to play the pedal and you will need to watch your child to make sure they are following the correct technique.

Their right foot heel should be on the ground when they press down on the pedal. I tell my students, pretend your heel is glued to the floor and can't let go the entire song. Even if the pedal lets go your heal is stuck!

Often when releasing the pedal, kids pick up their entire foot off the ground. This is incorrect technique and must be carefully watched for by you. Make sure their heel stays 'glued' to the floor when they release the pedal. If your child is young they may be too short to do this properly in the proper sitting posture. In that case, have them sit at the very edge of the bench. Don't sacrifice keeping the heal on the floor even if they are small.

Each part of the pedal mark in the image to the right has a specific meaning and instruction associated with it. The line at the front means to push down the pedal, the long line in the middle means to hold it down and the line at the end going up means to lift up the pedal. Remember during each of those steps the heel never leaves the floor.

DOWN   HOLD   UP

HAVING A STEADY BEAT

Make sure each in each song your child learns that they are keeping a steady beat. This means that the speed that they count their song never changes. There are not sections where they count faster or slower than others.

Let's say a song Is in 4/4 time and you do the counts 1-2-3-4 in each measure. Make sure each number is almost robotic in its delivery. If a section is easy, a student often counts very fast in that section, but when there is a hard part then suddenly the counting becomes very slow. This should never be the case. Have them practice it at a slow speed so the easy and the hard sections can be played at the same speed. Counting should never sound like:

1 *pause* **2-3** *pause* **4** *pause* **1-2** *pause* **3** *pause* **4-1** *pause* **2-3** *pause* **4**

Instead all numbers should be held for equal amounts of time and should sound like:

1-2-3-4-1-2-3-4-1-2-3-4

The most common spot for a pause if after the 4 before beat 1. The bar line tends to make kids pause. Make sure even going from beat 4 to beat 1 does not have a pause.

TEACHING THE PRACTICE SONG

The right hand is in C position with the 1 finger playing middle C.

The left hand has moved off of C position. First, ask your child is what note they see in the left hand. They should be able to identify that it is a B. This is a middle B right below middle C.

Now that they have found the correct note for the LH, they need to focus on the finger number that belongs on that note. It is the 1 finger on middle B. This means the thumbs on both your child's hands are on the notes right next to each other in the middle of the piano. Now that their hands are in place, they don't have to move again for the whole song.

Remember the steps to practice a song. First have them write in the counts and clap the rhythm hands apart before attempting to play the notes.

Point out the rest in the LH that occurs on beat 1. That means that the RH plays on beat 1 followed by the LH on beat 2-3-4 in measure 1 & 2.

Also discuss where the pedal plays in the song. Do not add in the pedal until all the notes and rhythms have been mastered. It should be the last step.

Daily Practice Log (4-6 days @ 15-20 minutes each day):
- *Flashcards for terms*
- *Flashcards for all notes (find the location on the piano for some of them)*
- *Practice song*
- *Corresponding Theory Chapter*
- *Hands together C Scale going up and down*
- *Identify bass, middle, treble C and D*

Stephanie Parker

PRACTICE SONG lesson 2: The Dreamy March

The Dreamy March

The Dreamy March

Practice song answer for parents... Don't let your child see this answer at any time.

LESSON 3

Start each lesson by going over each item in the previous weeks practice log. Repeat last weeks lesson if your child cannot complete their practice log independently including playing their homework practice song with approximately 85% accuracy. Do this at the beginning of each lesson the entire level.

HALF REST

The next term we will add to our flashcards is the half rest. A half rest is very similar to a half note. Both get 2 beats. A half note gets 2 beats holding down the note on the piano. A half rest gets 2 beats of silence. This is called a half rest and it gets 2 beats of silence (young children I suggest teaching them to keep the rest time by saying: shh-shh)

On the front of the flashcard draw the image to the right. On the back write half rest - 2 beats of silence.

The individual symbol is like the image above. However, as shown in the image to the right, when the half rest is placed in music the bottom line blends into the staff. You could draw this image on the flashcard as well so they can recognize the half rest by itself as well as in the staff.

As I'm sure you noticed, the half rest and whole rest look very similar. The whole rest looks like a whole in the ground and the box is facing down. With the half rest, the box is facing up.

Two help students not get confused, I teach students the trick that a half rest looks like a hat. Hat/half sound similar. A whole rest looks like a whole in the ground.

The image to the right shows the difference between the half rest and whole rest in music when placed side by side. Go over the difference in these rests with your child until it makes sense to

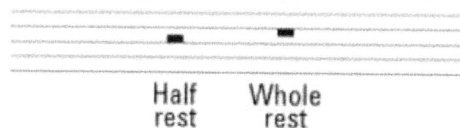

Half rest   Whole rest

them.

PLAYING IN CONTRARY MOTION

Your child has played the two hands simultaneously before. However, it has always been with both hands going in the same direction. For this weeks song, we will introduce two hands playing at the same time but moving in different directions.

Teach your child to break apart the music when learning a song. Is the right hand stepping or skipping? Is it going up or down? Then have them do the same for the left hand. Is the left hand stepping or skipping? Is it going up or down? Then have them follow those patterns.

Let's try some examples together before moving on to this weeks practice song. Look over the following two examples together and then have your child play each example. Each example has both hands in C position.

The hands in this example both move in the same direction.

The hands in this example both move in the opposite direction.

TEACHING THE PRACTICE SONG:

Neither hand is in C position for this song. Ask your child what the RH note is. If they struggle say "Is it a line or space note? What do the RH lines say?" That should lead them to answering note G for every **G**ood boy deserves fudge. Then have them put their 1 finger on that G.

The left hand has the first note of B. This is a memory flashcard. This is a middle B right below middle C. Notice that the music tells you to put your 2 finger on the B. This is so the 1 finger (thumb) will be free to play the C later in the song, so make sure 2 goes on B.

This song has a different time signature than the last 2 songs. This song is in 3/4 time so each measure will count 1-2-3. Have your child write in the counts and clap the rhythm before attempting to play the notes.

Daily Practice Log (4-6 days @ 15-20 minutes each day):
* *Flashcards for terms*
* *Flashcards for all notes (find the location on the piano for some of them)*
* *Practice song*
* *Corresponding Theory Chapter*
* *Hands together C Scale going up and down*
* *Identify bass, middle, treble C and D*

PRACTICE SONG lesson 3: Criss Cross Applesauce

Criss Cross Applesauce

ANSWERS FOR PARENTS

Criss Cross Applesauce

Practice song answer for parents... Don't let your child see this answer at any time.

LESSON 4

LEARNING ABOUT INTERVALS - The 2nd

Interval of a 2nd:

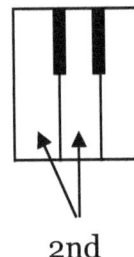

2nd

You have taught your child steps and skips in the previous book. There is another way to refer to steps and skips and that is with intervals. Intervals simply means how far apart two notes are on the piano or on the music.

When a music steps, that is called an interval of a 2nd. It means that the notes are 2 notes away from each other. Always count the note you start on as number 1 when counting intervals.

Interval of a 2nd:

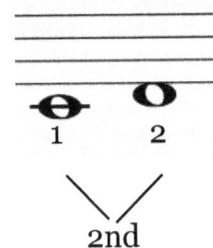

1   2

2nd

TREBLE CLEF LEDGER LINE FLASHCARDS

Your child daily practices their note flashcards and is hopefully getting very fast at them. It is time to add some new notes. We won't be playing these new notes in our songs for quite a while, but we want to have plenty of time to build a strong understanding of these notes with your child before attempting to play them. The image to the right shows the treble clef ledger line notes we will be learning this lesson.

Make a separate flashcard pile for the ledger line notes. Do not combine them with the regular note flashcards at this level. That would be too hard for a student at this level.

This means your child should have a pile of term flashcards, a pile regular note flashcards, a pile of treble clef ledger line flashcards, and, eventually, a pile of bass clef ledger line flashcards. Each pile is done separately.

This is a lot of flashcards, so I recommended doing a different pile at the beginning, at the middle and at the end of the lesson/practice time to make it less boring for your child. This is not the most fun part of piano, but it is extremely important!

The first ledger lines we will learn are the notes going above the treble clef. When reading ledger line flashcards it is important to remember the pattern of music. If it is a line to a line skip a letter. If it is a line to a space go to the very next letter. When doing this, the easiest place to begin is on the F from every good boy deserves **Fudge**.

Here are the 4 new ledger line flashcards to make. Draw the image on the front and write the letter note name on the back of the flashcard

Now that you have created the ledger line flashcards let me explain in more detail how to understand the answer to each flashcard instead of simply doing just rote memorization. For all the notes above it is helpful to have your child looking at their piano as they figure out the ledger line note. It is very hard for them to do these flashcards without having a keyboard in front of them for a frame of reference.

First identify the F line, fudge. Then, the very next spot is a space. A line to a space is a step. So going to the very next letter in the alphabet is G or stepping up from F is G.

First identify the F line, fudge. Then realize that the next note is another line note. A line to a line is a skip. So from F skip over a letter in the alphabet. So Skipping from F we land on A.

First identify the F line, fudge. Point out the line below the ledger line note your see. The line (**Fudge**) to that next line higher would be a skip or A. Then we step up one more note from A which makes us land on B.

First identify the F line, fudge. Point out that the ledger line note is another line. However it isn't the very next line. Theres a blank line in between. Starting on fudge we skip to the blank ledger line (A) then skip a second time from A to the note which is C.

TEACHING THE PRACTICE SONG:

Neither hand is in C position for this song. Ask your child what the RH note is. If they struggle say "Is it a line or a space? What do the RH lines say?" That should lead them to answering note G for every **G**ood boy deserves fudge. Then have them put their 1 finger on that G.

The left hand has the first note of middle C. This is a memory flashcard. Place your child's 1 finger (thumb) on middle C.

Notice the pattern starting in measure 2 of the RH having a whole note play while the LH has a rest on beat 1. Then that whole note holds for counts 1-2-3-4 during which the left hand plays AT THE SAME TIME. Then in the next measure the left hand has a whole note that holds while the RH plays.

Have your child write in the counts and clap the rhythm before attempting to play the notes.

> *Daily Practice Log (4-6 days @ 15-20 minutes each day):*
> * ✳ *Flashcards for terms*
> * ✳ *Flashcards for all notes (find the location on the piano for some of them)*
> * ✳ *Practice song*
> * ✳ *Corresponding Theory Chapter*
> * ✳ *Hands together C Scale going up and down*
> * ✳ *Flashcards Treble clef ledger lines we've learned so far*

Stephanie Parker

PRACTICE SONG lesson 4: The Hopping Frog

The Hopping Frog

The Hopping Frog

Practice song answer for parents... Don't let your child see this answer at any time.

LESSON 5

LEARNING ABOUT INTERVALS - The 3rd

Interval of a 3rd:

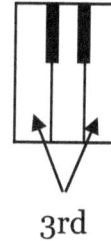

3rd

You taught your child last week that another way to refer to steps and skips is calling them intervals (how far apart are the notes). When counting intervals, always count the note you start on as number 1.

When two notes step (line to line or space to space), that is called an interval of a 2nd.

Interval of a 3rd:

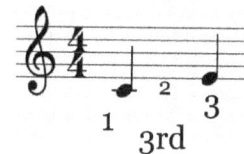

When two notes skip, that is called an interval of a 3rd. You started on the first note, skipped over the next note and landed on the 3rd. Or, as demonstrated in the example to the right, you started on the first Line (1), skipped over the space (2) and landed on the next line (3).

SHIFTING HANDS IN THE MIDDLE OF A SONG

Up until this point, when a hand found its position at the beginning of the song, it never moved the entire song. We will be introducing with this weeks song the concept of the hand moving in the middle of the song. This is always indicated with finger numbering showing a new position. However, as your child is getting used to this new concept there will be additional help in their music. For now, anytime you see the term "hand shift" above or below a finger number it is an extra indication showing your child to move to a new spot on the piano.

TEACHING THE PRACTICE SONG:

This song begins in C position for both hands. Before beginning, look over the song with your child for the locations a hand shift occurs. The first hand shift moves the right hand 1 finger to a G note. Then the second hand shift moves the RH back to C position. Have your child write in the counts and clap the rhythm before attempting to play the notes.

Daily Practice Log (4-6 days @ 15-20 minutes each day):
- ✳ *Flashcards for terms*
- ✳ *Flashcards for all notes (find the location on the piano for some of them)*
- ✳ *Practice song*
- ✳ *Corresponding Theory Chapter*
- ✳ *Hands together C Scale going up and down*
- ✳ *Flashcards Treble clef ledger lines we've learned so far*

4

PRACTICE SONG lesson 5: The Flower Pot

The Flower Pot

The Flower Pot

Practice song answer for parents... Don't let your child see this answer at any time.

LESSON 6

TREBLE CLEF LEDGER LINE FLASHCARDS

There are another set of ledger lines in the treble clef that go below the staff. Luckily you have already taught your child 2 of these notes: middle C and D. You can keep middle C and D in the normal note flashcards for that reason.

The two new flashcards we will add are the two notes below middle C as pictured in the image to the right. For these two notes it's easiest to find the empty ledger line that we are familiar with as middle C and count down from there.

The B one is directly below middle C so it is the note/letter before C. Make a ledger line flashcard for this with the front of the flashcard having the image to the right and on the back write B.

The A note is the ledger line below middle C (a line to line skip). If you find middle C on the piano and skip down you will land on an A. Make a ledger line flashcard for this with the front of the flashcard having the image to the right and on the back write A.

Add these two new flashcards to the other ledger line flashcard pile and practice them all together when you practice the treble clef ledger lines.

TEACHING THE PRACTICE SONG:

This song begins in C position for both hands and there is no hand shift.

Make sure to have your child write in the counts for this song and count it aloud. There are 2 ties that hold over the bar line and that can be a very tricky rhythm. Make sure they master it with clapping and then make sure they play that part of the rhythm correctly too.

Also notice the contrary motion in the second to last measure (measure 10).

At the end of measure 4, there is a repeat sign. Point to it and ask your child what its name is and what it means. When they get to the repeat the first time they should repeat back to the beginning of the song. When they get to the repeat sign the second time they ignore it and keep going on to measure 5.

Daily Practice Log (4-6 days @ 15-20 minutes each day):
* ❇ *Flashcards for terms*
* ❇ *Flashcards for all notes (find the location on the piano for some of them)*
* ❇ *Practice song*
* ❇ *Corresponding Theory Chapter*
* ❇ *Hands together C Scale going up and down*
* ❇ *Flashcards Treble clef ledger lines we've learned so far*

PRACTICE SONG lesson 6: A Happy Day

A Happy Day

A Happy Day

Practice song answer for parents... Don't let your child see this answer at any time.

CHAPTER 2: The G Scale

LESSON 1

THE G SCALE - RIGHT HAND GOING UP

Your child has learned the C scale and can play it hands together going up and down. The next scale we will learn is the G scale. The G scale uses the exact same fingering as the C scale.

There are two differences between the C scale and the G scale. The first difference is the starting note in both hands is now a G. The second difference is there are not all white notes in the G scale. There is an F#. So, instead of playing a white note F, your child will need to play a F#.

The image to the right shows what the G major scale looks like on the piano and which notes are played in the G scale.

This week have your child play the right hand G scale going up only. Below are the notes and fingering for this scale in the Right hand going up. The large number is where the thumb tunnels under the 3.

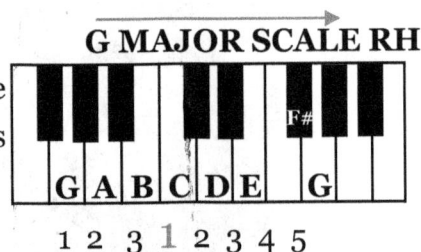

G MAJOR SCALE RH

G A B C D E G

1 2 3 1 2 3 4 5

LEARNING ABOUT INTERVALS - The 4th

You taught your child that another way to refer to steps and skips is calling them an intervals (how far apart are the notes). When counting intervals, always count the note you start on as number 1.

When two notes step, that is called an interval of a 2nd.
When two notes skip, that is called an interval of a 3rd.

When two notes skip plus one more step that is called a 4th. As demonstrated in the example to the right, you started on the first Line (1), skip over the space (2nd) to the next line (3rd) plus one additional space (4th).

Interval of a 4th:

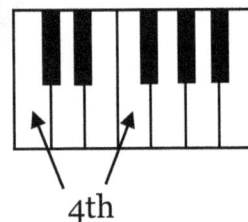

4th

Interval of a 4th:

4th

TEACHING THE PRACTICE SONG:

This song begins on an F note in both hands. Place the 1 finger on F above middle C in the RH and the 5 finger on the F below middle C in the left hand.

This song is all skips with no steps. When the hands play together in this song (measure 6,7,8), they move in the same direction. However, take note that they are playing different notes from one another as they skip up and skip down.

Make sure to have your child write in the counts for this song and count it aloud. Especially have your child pay attention to the dotted half note which we haven't used in our songs in a little while.

Review what the dynamics markings (*p, mf, f*) mean and point out those markings in the song. Wait to have them incorporate the dynamics into playing their song until they have mastered the notes and rhythms. It should be a last step of their practice.

Daily Practice Log (4-6 days @ 15-20 minutes each day):
- ✸ *Flashcards for terms*
- ✸ *Flashcards for all notes (find the location on the piano for some of them)*
- ✸ *Practice song*
- ✸ *Corresponding Theory Chapter*
- ✸ *Hands together C Scale going up and down*
- ✸ *Flashcards Treble clef ledger lines we've learned so far*
- ✸ *G scale RH going up*

A Sweet Face

ANSWERS FOR PARENTS

A Sweet Face

Practice song answer for parents... Don't let your child see this answer at any time.

LESSON 2

THE G SCALE - RIGHT HAND GOING UP AND DOWN

To learn the scale heading in the downward direction first have your child go up the scale and hold the G at the top. Then have them go back down.

The finger pattern for going down the scale is the exact same finger pattern for the C scale heading down.

Below are the notes and fingering for this scale in the Right hand going down. The large number is where the bunny hops over the 1.

G MAJOR SCALE RH

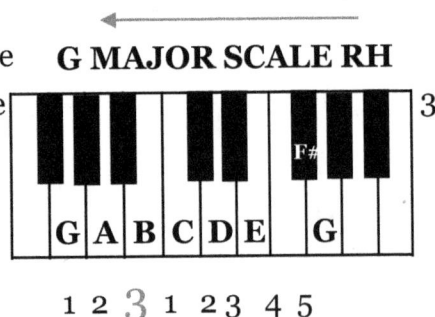

G A B C D E G

1 2 3 1 2 3 4 5

Once that makes sense to your child have your child practice independently going up and down the G scale.

GOING UP   G-A-B-C-D-E-F#-G

                  1 2 3 1 2 3 4 5

GOING DOWN   G-F#-E-D-C-B-A-G

                  5 4 3 2 1 3 2 1

Interval of a 5th:

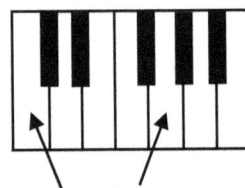

Interval of a 5th:

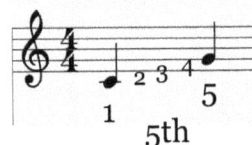

LEARNING ABOUT INTERVALS - The 5th

You taught your child that another way to refer to steps and skips is calling them an interval (how far apart are the notes). When counting intervals always count the note you start on as number 1.

When two notes step, that is called an interval of a 2nd.
When two notes skip, that is called an interval of a 3rd.
When two notes skip plus 1 more note that's called an interval of a 4th.

When a note skips 2 times that is an interval of a 5th.
Based on the example to the right, start on the first note,
skip to the empty line note (3rd) and then skip a second time to the next line note (5th).

TEACHING THE PRACTICE SONG:

This song begins in C position for both hands; however, there is a hand shift that occurs on the second line in the right hand only. The left hand does not move.

Make sure to have your child write in the counts for this song and count it aloud with clapping before attempting to play it. Notice the ties in line 1 and 2 and make sure they're clapping reflects holding the note over the bar line.

Have them play the slurs in the last line legato. Also pay attention to the dynamic markings throughout the piece. Review what the dynamics markings (*p, mf, f*) mean. Wait to have them incorporate the dynamics into their song until they have mastered the notes and rhythms. It should be a last step of their practice.

Daily Practice Log (4-6 days @ 15-20 minutes each day):
 * *Flashcards for terms*
 * *Flashcards for all notes (find the location on the piano for some of them)*
 * *Practice song*
 * *Corresponding Theory Chapter*
 * *Hands together C Scale going up and down*
 * *Flashcards all treble clef ledger lines combined*
 * *G scale RH going up and down*

PRACTICE SONG lesson 2: Sleepy Jack

Sleepy Jack

ANSWERS FOR PARENTS

Sleepy Jack

Practice song answer for parents... Don't let your child see this answer at any time:

LESSON 3

THE G SCALE - LEFT HAND GOING UP

The left hand G scale follows the same pattern as the LH
C scale. That means your fingering going up will be
5-4-3-2-1-3-2-1.

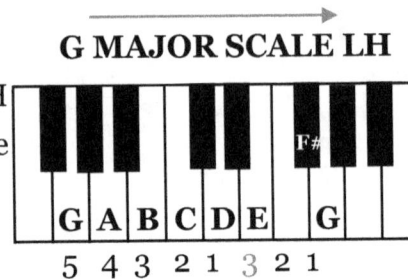

G MAJOR SCALE LH

Below are the notes and fingering for this scale in the
left hand going up. The large number is where the 3 bunny hops over the 1.

G-A-B-C-D-E-F#-G

5 4 3 2 1 3 2 1

LEARNING ABOUT INTERVALS - The 4th & 5th

You taught your child that another way to refer to steps and skips is calling them an
interval (how far apart are the notes). When counting intervals, always count the note you
start on as number 1.

When two notes step, that is called an interval of a 2nd. When two notes skip, that is
called an interval of a 3rd. When two notes skip plus 1 that's an interval of a 4th. When
two notes skip and skip again that's an interval of a 5th.

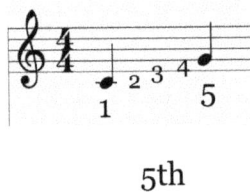

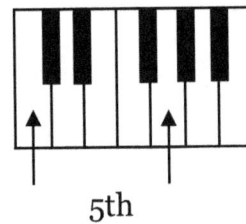

Look at these examples of intervals of a 4th and 5th side by side.

Interval of a 4th:

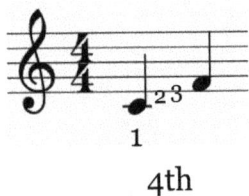

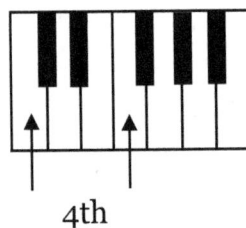

Interval of a 5th:

Interval of a 4th:

Interval of a 5th:

4th

5th

4th

5th

TEACHING THE PRACTICE SONG:

This song begins on a D note for both hands. The right hand has a 1 finger on the D above middle C and the left hand has a 5 finger on the D above bass C.

Make sure to have your child write in the counts for this song and count it aloud with clapping before attempting to play it. Notice all the quarter rests. Make sure you child gives 1 full beat of silence, or shh, during each rest.

After your child has an understanding of the notes and rhythms, add in the dynamics. The dynamics in this song start *mf* and grow to *f*.

Notice the left hand, measures 15 & 16, uses the interval of a 4th going down. Show your child this interval before they begin playing. Point out to them how, from the first note, it skips to the next line plus one more space making it a 4th. On the piano, they play the first note (an A) and then count that as number one and count to 4 landing them on an E.

Daily Practice Log (4-6 days @ 15-20 minutes each day):
* *Flashcards for terms*
* *Flashcards for all notes (find the location on the piano for some of them)*
* *Practice song*
* *Corresponding Theory Chapter*
* *Hands together C Scale going up and down*
* *Flashcards all treble clef ledger lines combined*
* *RH G scale going up and down*
* *LH G scale going up and down*

PRACTICE SONG lesson 3: Arabian Dance

Arabian Dance

ANSWERS FOR PARENTS

Arabian Dance

Practice song answer for parents... Don't let your child see this answer at any time:

LESSON 4

THE G SCALE - LEFT HAND UP AND DOWN

To learn the scale heading in the downward direction in the left hand, first have your child go up the scale and hold the G at the top, then have them go back down.

The finger pattern for the LH going down the scale is the exact same finger patter for the LH C scale heading down.

Below are the notes and fingering for this scale in the left hand going down. The large number is where the 1 finger tunnels under the 3 finger.

G MAJOR SCALE LH

G-F#-E-D-C-B-A-G

1 2 3 1 2 3 4 5

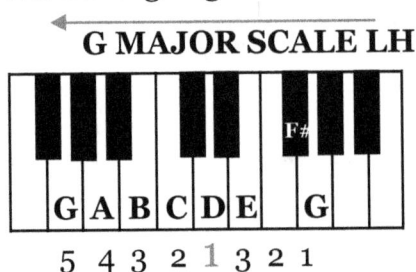

Once that makes sense to your child, have your child practice independently going up and down the G scale in the left hand.

GOING UP   G-A-B-C-D-E-F#-G

                               5 4 3 2 1 3 2 1

GOING DOWN   G-F#-E-D-C-B-A-G

                               1 2 3 1 2 3 4 5

LEARNING ABOUT INTERVALS - The 2nd, 3rd, 4th, 5th

You taught your child last week that another way to refer to steps and skips is calling them an interval (how far apart are the notes). When counting intervals, always count the note you start on as number 1.

Now we will begin to identify 2nds, 3rds, 4ths, 5ths all together.

When two notes step, that is called an interval of a 2nd.

When two notes skip, that is called an interval of a 3rd.

When two notes skip plus 1 more that is called an interval of a 4th.

When two notes skip and skip again that is called an interval of a 5th.

Study the image below until your child can tell the difference between 2nds, 3rds, 4th and 5ths.

Interval of a 2nd: **Interval of a 3rd:**   **Interval of a 4th:**   **Interval of a 5th:**

Interval of a 2nd: **Interval of a 3rd:**   **Interval of a 4th:**   **Interval of a 5th:**

TEACHING THE PRACTICE SONG:

This song starts both hands on C position and stays C position for the whole song. It is easier positioning so you can help your child focus on playing the intervals of 4th and 5ths.

Make sure to have your child write in the counts for this song and counts it aloud with clapping before attempting to play it. Notice the song is in 3/4 time.

Point out to your child the interval of a 3rd throughout the song. From the 3rd we figure out if the next note or notes are a 4th or a 5th. From the 3rd (skip) did it go up 1 which would be a 4th or from the 3rd (skip) did it skip again which would be a 5th.

Notice that the RH skips up to 3rds, 4ths and 5ths, but the LH skips down to the 3rds, 4ths and 5ths.

Daily Practice Log (4-6 days @ 15-20 minutes each day):
- ❋ *Flashcards for terms*
- ❋ *Flashcards for all notes (find the location on the piano for some of them)*
- ❋ *Practice song*
- ❋ *Corresponding Theory Chapter*
- ❋ *Hands together C Scale going up and down*
- ❋ *Flashcards all treble clef ledger lines combined*
- ❋ *G Scale RH going up and down*
- ❋ *G Scale LH going up and down*

PRACTICE SONG lesson 4: Together4ever

Together4ever

Together4ever

Practice song answer for parents... Don't let your child see this answer at any time:

LESSON 5

G SCALE HANDS TOGETHER

You have taught your child to play the G scale hands apart. If they still struggle hands apart, really focus on the scale practice hands apart so they can master it and move on to this step of playing the G scale in both hands at the same time.

Before beginning, remind your child that even though they're starting on G, it will be the exact same fingering as the C scale. Also, remind your child that, when playing a scale hands together, both of the hands do the exact same thing, but in reverse of each other. So going up the scale the right hand will be tunneling under the 3 finger and the left hand will have the 3rd finger hopping over.

Here is what that will look like:

	G	A	B	C	D	E	F#	G
RIGHT HAND:	1	2	3	1	2	3	4	5
LEFT HAND:	5	4	3	2	1	3	2	1

Notice that the "tunnel" and the "bunny hop" do not happen at the exact same time. First comes the tunnel followed two notes later by the bunny hop.

When teaching this to your child, take it slow. Have them play just the G's together. Once they do that with ease, then have them play G's to A's together. Once that happens, have them do the first 3 notes together.

This is where it'll get harder. While both hands are on the B note have them just hold the note down and really talk through what will happen next. Next the left hand will play the 2 finger on the C, but the right hand will have the thumb tunnel under to the C.

When they master playing the C's together, pause. Make sure they shifted their whole right hand in line with the new thumb position. If everything looks right move on to the D's together which is pretty simple.

Here comes the bunny hop. While holding the D's down in both hands have the LH 3 finger bunny hop over the thumb. Once its in position to play the E have both hands play the E's together simultaneously. Then, shift the left hand to be in line with the new position of the third finger.

Your Child's hand is in position and ready to play the F#'s together and then the G's together. Just make sure they play F# and not the F white note.

Stop here. Don't try and go down the scale yet. Do this a couple more times throughout the lesson until you're sure you child will be able to practice it during the week.

At this stage, do not have your child go straight to hands together practice each day with the G scale. Have them play the right hand scale up and down, then the left hand scale up and down. Then have them do hands together going up only.

NOTE HEAD STEM DIRECTION

You may have noticed that sometimes a note has a stem going down on the left side of the note and sometimes there is a stem going up on the right side of the note. There is a reason for this.

Notes that are BELOW line 3 on the staff have stems going up on the right side like the image to the right.

Notes that are ON or ABOVE line 3 have stems going down on the left side like the image to the right.

This rule applies to both the treble and bass clef notes.

TEACHING THE PRACTICE SONG:

This song starts both hands on C position. Show your child that the left hand alternates 4ths and 5th intervals with 2 notes playing at once and the right hand plays 4ths and 5ths intervals one note at a time. Have them identify is it a skip plus one (a 4th) or a skip and skip again (a 5th).

Make sure to have your child write in the counts for this song and count it aloud with clapping before attempting to play it. Be careful that your child observes all the rests and doesn't hold the note through the rest. Review with them which kind of rest it is in measure 5 (a half rest worth 2 beats).

There is a hand shift in this song. This time, not only does one hand shift, but both hands shift at the same time. Teach your child to use the time during the measure 5 half rest to shift their hands and be ready and waiting for the notes in measure 6.

The right hand shifts up to 1 finger on G. The left hand also moves to G but with the 4th finger. In the left hand, the 4th and 2nd finger will be playing 2 notes simultaneously In measure 6. The 4th and 1st finger will be playing the 2 notes simultaneously in the following measure (measure 7). That pattern repeats in measure 8 & 9.

Daily Practice Log (4-6 days @ 15-20 minutes each day):
- ❋ *Flashcards for terms*
- ❋ *Flashcards for all notes (find the location on the piano for some of them)*
- ❋ *Practice song*
- ❋ *Corresponding Theory Chapter*
- ❋ *Hands together C Scale going up and down*
- ❋ *Flashcards all treble clef ledger lines combined*
- ❋ *G Scale RH going up and down*
- ❋ *G Scale LH going up and down*
- ❋ *Hands together G sale going up only*

PRACTICE SONG lesson 5: The Drummer's March

The Drummer's March

ANSWERS FOR PARENTS

The Drummer's March

Practice song answer for parents... Don't let your child see this answer at any time:

LESSON 6

G SCALE HANDS TOGETHER GOING UP AND DOWN

If your child is able to go up the G scale hands together, then move on to teaching them this week about coming back down the scale. If going up the scale hands together is still a challenge for them, give them another week or two just going up hands together and then at that time return to this part of lesson 6.

Just like when they went up the scale the two hands did the opposite of one another (one tunneled and the other one bunny hopped), the same thing will happen going down except the two hands will switch which one they're doing.

On the way down, the right hand will bunny hop when it runs out of fingers and the left hand will tunnel under after the 3 finger.

The best way to teach going down the scale is to have them go up the scale hands together and stop when they get to the top on that G and rest there. Now you will talk them through each note.

For the first two notes, their fingers are exactly where they should be just don't forget the F#. So have them go down playing the F#'s together then the E's together and then have them pause holding down the E's.

On the E, the left hand is on the 3 finger, so it will need to have the 1 finger (thumb) tunnel under to the D. Once its in position, have BOTH hands play the D's at the same time and then shift the left hand to be in position with the new thumb location.

C's together is next and is fairly simple, but it means the right hand has run out of fingers. This means the right hand now needs to have the 3rd finger bunny hop over the thumb and get into position to play the B. Once it's in position have the two hands play the B's at the same time. Then have the right hand shift the hand so its in position with the new location of the 3rd finger.

The last two notes are all lined up and ready to go, so have them play the A's then the G's together.

If your child catches on to this concept fairly quickly, they can go straight to hands together G scale in their practice time. If it is a bit of a struggle still, then have their scale practice time be:

1) RH only G scale up and down
2) LH only G scale up and down
3) Hands together G scale up and down.

TEACHING THE PRACTICE SONG:

This song has both hands on C position for the whole song.

Show your child that the whole song is intervals of a 3rd. They are all skips. But the skips step up and down each measure to a new starting note.

On the third line show your child how the skips of 3rds between the two hands stop mirroring each other and begin moving in contrary motion.

Make sure to have your child write in the counts for this song and count it aloud with clapping before attempting to play it. Point out to your child that we are in 3/4 time.

Daily Practice Log (4-6 days @ 15-20 minutes each day):
* ✸ *Flashcards for terms*
* ✸ *Flashcards for all notes (find the location on the piano for some of them)*
* ✸ *Practice song*
* ✸ *Corresponding Theory Chapter*
* ✸ *Hands together C & G Scale going up and down*
* ✸ *Flashcards all treble clef ledger lines combined*

PRACTICE SONG lesson 6: Flying Kites

Flying kites

Practice song answer for parents... Don't let your child see this answer at any time:

ANSWERS FOR PARENTS

Flying kites

CHAPTER 3: Learning Major Chords

LESSON 1

LEARNING MAJOR CHORDS - C MAJOR

For this level, all references to playing chords should be played with the RIGHT hand. We will learn to play chords with the left hand later.

Major chords are an incredibly important part of piano. Understanding major chords will make playing classical music easier. Also, those students who want to learn to read popular music or church music will need to have a strong foundation in chords.

A major chord has 3 notes that are played simultaneously. The first note that is played is the name of the chord. So we are learning about the C major chord which means our first note will be a C.

The next note that is played is a skip above the first note. Since our first note is C, a skip above C is an E. This is demonstrated in the image to the right.

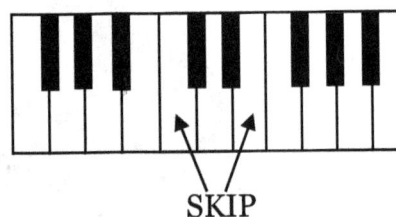

Another way to find the 2nd note of a chord is to skip 3 half steps (We will go over half steps more later. A 1/2 step just means the notes as close together as possibly including the black notes. Basically count everything). This is demonstrated in the image to the right.

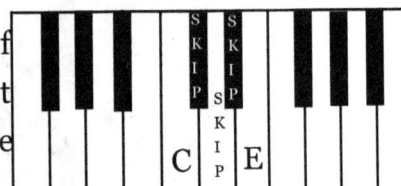

Have your child play a RH C and hold it down. While their C is holding down, have them find the skip above it (E) and play the E. Then have them pick up their hand and play the C and the E AT THE SAME TIME.

After the E, there is one more note they need to find. That is the 3rd note of the chord.

To find the 3rd note of the chord, you start on the second note (E) and skip up again. In this case, a skip above E is a G. A chord is made up of all skips. You find the first note (The name of the chord) then you skip (that's your second note) and then you skip again (that's your 3rd note). Then you play all those notes at the exact same time. **It is not a chord**

unless it is played at the exact same time. This is demonstrated in the image to the right.

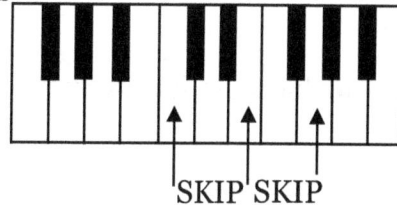

Another way to find the 3rd note of the chord is to skip 2 half steps. So the formula for any major chords is skip 3 notes skip 2 notes. This is demonstrated in the image to the right.

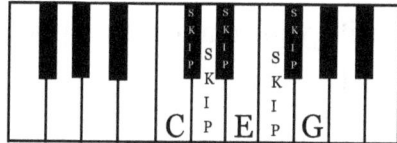

With their right hand, Have your child play and hold a C, E AND G note all at the same time. Make sure they use the 1 - 3 - 5 fingers when doing this. This is a C chord! Make sure no extra notes are playing.

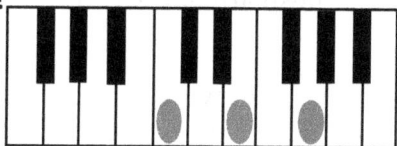

Many new students struggle to play all 3 notes simultaneously with curved fingers. Really focus on this skill until it is mastered.

Don't just have them memorize the letters of the chord. Make sure they understand the why behind it.

PLAYING THE BASS, MIDDLE, AND TREBLE NOTES ON THE PIANO

We have been identifying in our theory the bass, middle and treble notes on the piano for many weeks. Now it is time apply that concept in our songs.

Take out the C flashcards that match the notes to the right. Have your child play the C in the right location on piano as they see the flashcard.

Our music will begin to utilize the notes in different locations so help your child pay close attention from here on out not just to the note names, but to their location on the staff so they can play the correct correlating location on the piano.

TEACHING THE PRACTICE SONG:

This song has both hands start on C position.

The song has quite a few hand shifts, but for the first time we are shifting to treble C & D.

Talk with your child before playing the song about which location on the piano each hand shift is located at. Ask them if each RH hand shift is at middle or treble C or D.

There are two hand shifts in the left hand, but this is to the bass D and then back down to bass C. These are notes your child should be familiar with identifying.

Make sure to have your child write in the counts for this song and count it aloud with clapping before attempting to play it. Point out the ties in the right hand that hold while the left hand plays.

Daily Practice Log (4-6 days @ 15-20 minutes each day):
* *Flashcards for terms*
* *Flashcards for all notes (find the location on the piano for some of them)*
* *Practice song*
* *Corresponding Theory Chapter*
* *Hands together C & G Scale going up and down*
* *Flashcards all treble clef ledger lines combined*
* *Play C major chord*

Stephanie Parker

PRACTICE SONG lesson 1: Walking on the Moon

Walking on the Moon

Walking on the Moon

Practice song answer for parents... Don't let your child see this answer at any time:

LESSON 2

BASS CLEF LEDGER LINE FLASHCARDS

Your child daily practices their note flashcards and their treble clef ledger line flashcards. It is time to add some new notes. We won't be playing these new notes in our songs for quite a while, but we want to have plenty of time to build a strong understanding of these notes with your child before attempting to play them.

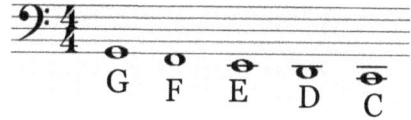

Make a separate flashcard pile for the bass clef ledger line notes. Keep them separate from the treble clef ledger line flashcards during this level. Next level we will combine the two clef ledger lines. Also, do not combine them with the regular note flashcards at this level. That would be too hard for a student at this level.

This means your child should have a pile of term flashcards, a pile of regular note flashcards, a pile of treble clef ledger line flashcards, and a pile of bass clef ledger line flashcards. Each pile is done separately.

This is a lot of flashcards, so I recommended doing a different pile at the beginning, at the middle and at the end of the lesson/practice time to make it less boring for your child. This is not the most fun part of piano, but it is extremely important!

The first bass clef ledger lines we will learn are the notes going below the bass clef. When reading ledger line flashcards, it is important to remember the pattern of music. If it is a line to a line, skip a letter. If it is a line to a space go to the very next letter. When doing this, the easiest place to begin is on the bottom line G for Grizzly bears don't fly airplanes.

Here are the new ledger line flashcards to make. Draw the image on the front and write the letter note name on the back of the flashcard

Now that you have created the ledger line flashcards let me explain in more detail how to understand the answer instead of simply doing just rote memorization.

For all the notes below it is helpful to have your child looking at their piano as they figure out the ledger line note. It is very hard for them to do without having a keyboard in front of them for a frame of reference.

First, identify the G line, "grizzly." Then the very next spot is a space. A line to a space is a step DOWN. Going to the letter in the alphabet right before F is G or stepping down from G is F.

First, identify the G line, "grizzly." Then realize that the next note you see is another line note. A line to a line is a skip, but it's a skip down so we have to go backwards in our alphabet. From G, skip over a letter in the alphabet going backwards. Skipping from G we land on E.

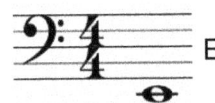

First, identify the G line, "grizzly." Point out the line below the ledger line note your see. The first line (G-grizzly) to that black line below it would be a skip down or E. But that's not where our note is at. We then step down one more note from E which makes us land on D.

First, identify the G line, "grizzly." Point out that the ledger line note we see is another line. However it isn't the very next ledger line. Theres a blank line in between. So starting on G (grizzly) we skip down to the blank ledger line (E) then skip a second time from E to the note which is C.

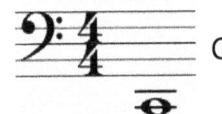

TEACHING THE PRACTICE SONG:

This song feels like it is in C position, but it actually is not. The left Hand is in C position, but the right hand is on the C above middle C, treble C. So, it is technically not in the traditional C position.

This song has a lot of rests so the left hand comes in on unusual beats within the measure. Make sure to have your child write in the counts for this song and count it aloud with clapping before attempting to play it accounting for the tricky rests in the left hand.

Each time the left hand comes in on beat 3, it has contrary motion with the right hand. Point out to your child that the left hand is stepping up while the right hand is stepping down in those locations.

Daily Practice Log (4-6 days @ 15-20 minutes each day):
- ✳ *Flashcards for terms*
- ✳ *Flashcards for all notes (find the location on the piano for some of them)*
- ✳ *Practice song*
- ✳ *Corresponding Theory Chapter*
- ✳ *Hands together C & G Scale going up and down*
- ✳ *Flashcards all treble clef ledger lines combined*
- ✳ *Flashcard bass clef ledger line notes learned this lesson*
- ✳ *Play C major chord*

PRACTICE SONG lesson 2: The Vineyard

The Vineyard

Stephanie Parker

ANSWERS FOR PARENTS

The Vineyard

Practice song answer for parents... Don't let your child see this answer at any time:

LESSON 3

LEARNING MAJOR CHORDS - F MAJOR

Your child has been playing the C major chord for a couple of weeks, now it's time to add the F major chord to their practice time.

The first note that is played in any chord is the letter name of the chord. We are learning about the F major chord which means our first note will be a F.

Using the skip method The next note that is played is a skip above the first note. Since our first note is F, a skip above F is an A. From that A note we determine our 3rd note by skipping yet again. From the second note (A) we skip and land on the note C. This is demonstrated in the image to the right.

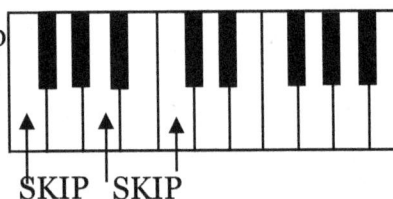

Using the alternative way to find the 2nd & 3rd notes of a chord is to skip 3 half steps to find the 2nd note. Then skip 2 half steps to find the 3rd note. This is demonstrated in the image to the right.

Have your child play a F, A AND C note all at the same time in their RIGHT hand. Make sure they use the 1 - 3 - 5 fingers when doing this. This is a F chord and is demonstrated in the image to the right.

Remember, it's not a chord unless all the notes are played at the exact same time.

Just like for the C chord, don't just have them memorize the letters of the chord. Make sure they understand the why behind it.

FERMATA

The next term we will add to our flashcards this level is fermata. A fermata (pronounced fir-mah-tah) is placed over a single note. When you see a fermata over a note it means to hold that note extra time. It isn't specific how much longer to hold the note. Just give it extra time. On the front of the flashcard, draw the image to the right. On the back of the flashcard write fermata - to hole the note longer than you are supposed to.

TEACHING THE PRACTICE SONG:

This song has the right hand 1 finger on treble C until measure 9 where the hand shifts. Have your child figure out what note it moves to. They should say the A above middle C with the 4th finger. On the last line the right hand moves back to its original position.

The left hand has its 3rd finger on the F note and it stays in that position the entire song. Show your child that the first two lines of the song is all different intervals. Measure 1 is 4ths, measure 2 is 3rds, measure 3 is 2nds and measure 4 is 4ths going down. That pattern repeats on the 2nd and the last line. Make sure to have your child write in the counts for this song and count it aloud with clapping before attempting to play it. Point out to your child that we are in 3/4 time.

Daily Practice Log (4-6 days @ 15-20 minutes each day):
* *Flashcards for terms*
* *Flashcards for all notes (find the location on the piano for some of them)*
* *Practice song*
* *Corresponding Theory Chapter*
* *Hands together C & G Scale going up and down*
* *Flashcards all treble clef ledger lines combined*
* *Flashcard bass clef ledger line notes learned last lesson*
* *Play C & F major chord*

PRACTICE SONG lesson 3: The Mist

The Mist

*Hand
Shift*

*Hand
Shift*

Stephanie Parker

The Mist

Practice song answer for parents... Don't let your child see this answer at any time:

LESSON 4

BASS CLEF LEDGER LINE FLASHCARDS

There are another set of ledger lines in the bass clef that go above the staff. Luckily you have already taught your child 2 of these notes: middle C and B. You can keep middle C and B in the normal note flashcards for that reason.

The two new flashcards we will add are the two notes above middle C as pictured in the image above. For these two notes, it's easiest to find the empty ledger line that we are familiar with as middle C and count up from there.

The D note is directly above middle C so it is the note/letter after C. Make a ledger line flashcard for this with the front of the flashcard having the image to the right and on the back write D.

The E note is the ledger line above middle C so if you find middle C on the piano and skip up you will land on an E. Make a ledger line flashcard for this with the front of the flashcard having the image to the right and on the back write A.

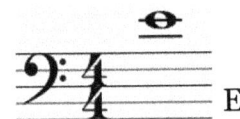

Add these two new flashcards to the other bass clef ledger line flashcard pile and practice them all together when you practice ledger lines.

RIT.

The next term we will add to our flashcards is RIT. RIT stands for the word ritardando (Pronounced ree-tar-dan-doh). When you see a ritardando in music from that point until the end the music gradually gets slower and slower.

I tell my students, think of the energizer bunny video. At first the energizer bunny is going at a good speed, but then as his battery runs out he walks and talks slower and slower until he eventually comes to a stop. A ritardando is like that. When you see it, pretend like you are running out of batteries and your counting of the song is getting slower and slower.

A ritardando is different than a fermata because a fermata means to only hold a single note longer; whereas, a ritardando means to slow down a whole section gradually.

On the front of the flashcard write RIT. On the back of the flashcard write ritardando - to gradually slow down.

TEACHING THE PRACTICE SONG:

This song has both hands on C position for the whole song.

This song is all about different intervals. Go through this song note by note with your child and have them identify if each group of notes is an interval of a 2nd, 3rd, 4th or 5th.

A great way to teach music that has groups of notes that change so frequently is show them to look for what stays the same and then also for for changes.

For example, in the right hand, the middle C on the bottom of each group of notes doesn't change even one time. Middle C always plays. It is the top note that moves. The top note in the RH steps up and down on the first line. On the second line the top note skips from a G to an E in measures 5 & 6 and then in measure 7 the top line begins stepping up and down again.

The left hand uses the same pattern except the top note is the one that stays the same almost the entire song. The G in the top note of the left hand plays almost the entire song except in measures 5 & 6 where the top note skips down to E.

Notice all the quarter rests in the first line. The rest alternate after every group of notes. Also notice that the RH and LH do not play at the same time at all during this song. It will alternate LH - RH - LH - RH etc. until measure 5. Review with your child in the music where the hands will play together and where they will play at separate times.

Make sure to have your child write in the counts for this song and count it aloud with clapping before attempting to play it.

Really analyze the music verbally about all the elements listed above before they attempt to play it. This song is more challenging and should definitely be learned and mastered hands apart before your child begins hand together practice.

Daily Practice Log (4-6 days @ 15-20 minutes each day):
* *Flashcards for terms*
* *Flashcards for all notes (find the location on the piano for some of them)*
* *Practice song*
* *Corresponding Theory Chapter*
* *Hands together C & G Scale going up and down*
* *Flashcards all treble clef ledger lines combined*
* *Flashcard bass clef ledger line notes combined*
* *Play C & F major chord*

Stephanie Parker

PRACTICE SONG lesson 4: Jumping Jacks

Jumping Jacks

Jumping Jacks

Practice song answer for parents... Don't let your child see this answer at any time:

LESSON 5

LEARNING MAJOR CHORDS - G MAJOR

Your child has been playing the C & F major chords for a couple of weeks, so now it's time to add the G major chord to their practice time.

The first note that is played in any chord is the letter name of the chord. We are learning about the G major chord which means our first note will be a G.

Using the skip method The next note that is played is a skip above the first note. Since our first note is G, a skip above G is an B. From that B note we determine our 3rd note by skipping yet again. So from the second note (B) we skip and land on the note D. This is demonstrated in the image to the right.

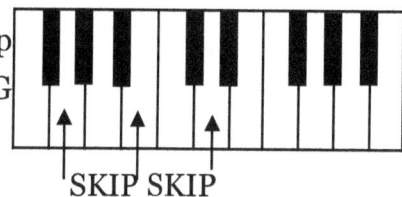

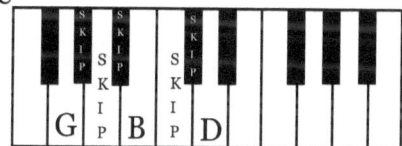

Using the alternative way to find the 2nd & 3rd notes of a chord is to skip 3 half steps to find the 2nd note. Then skip 2 half steps to find the 3rd note. This is demonstrated in the image to the right.

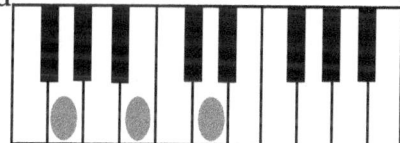

Have your child play a G, B AND D notes all at the same time in their RIGHT hand. Make sure they use the 1 - 3 - 5 fingers when doing this. This is a G chord and is demonstrated in the image to the right.

Remember, its not a chord unless all the notes are played at the exact same time.

Just like for the C & F chord, Don't just have them memorize the letters of the chord. Make sure they understand the why behind it.

PLAYING WITH THE LH CROSSING *OVER* THE RIGHT

Up until this point, all your child's music has had their left hand playing on the left side of their body and their right hand playing on the right side of their body.

I know it seems counter intuitive, but that will not always be the case. Sometimes the left hand crosses over the right and plays above the right hand.

This will be shown in the music by writing it into the music. For now, it will be very clearly marked in the music when the LH should cross over the RH and play above it. There will be arrows pointing to the note that crosses over and "PLAY LH" written into the musical score.

After the LH plays the note that crossed over, it should return to its normal position at the bottom of the piano. Have your child play the example below that demonstrates this. For this example start with both hands in C position and then the left hand crosses over the right hand to play the last note.

TEACHING THE PRACTICE SONG:

The right hand is in C position the whole song. The Left hand uses the 2 finger for every note except for in the 3rd line. When it plays the bottom note and when it crosses over the right hand it should be using the 2 finger for both of those.

Each left hand cross over note is either landing on a treble C or a treble D. Have your child identify which it is in each measure before playing.

Also notice the pedal at the beginning of each line. Do not have your child add in the pedal until they master all the other concepts in the song.

Daily Practice Log (4-6 days @ 15-20 minutes each day):

* ❋ *Flashcards for terms*
* ❋ *Flashcards for all notes (find the location on the piano for some of them)*
* ❋ *Practice song*
* ❋ *Corresponding Theory Chapter*
* ❋ *Hands together C & G Scale going up and down*
* ❋ *Flashcards all treble clef ledger lines combined*
* ❋ *Flashcard bass clef ledger line notes combined*
* ❋ *Play C & F & G major chord*

PRACTICE SONG lesson 5: The Floating Balloon

The Floating Balloon

ANSWERS FOR PARENTS

The Floating Balloon

Practice song answer for parents... Don't let your child see this answer at any time:

LESSON 6

PLAYING WITH THE RH CROSSING *OVER* THE LEFT

You taught your child in the last lesson that the left hand can cross over the right hand and play above the the right hand. The same thing can happen where the right hand can cross over the left hand and play below the left hand.

This will be shown in the music by writing it into the music. For now, it will be very clearly marked in the music when the RH should cross **over** the LH and play below it with arrows pointing to the note that crosses over and "PLAY RH" written into the musical score.

After the RH plays the note that crosses over, it should return to its normal position at the top of the piano. Have your child play the example below that demonstrates this.

PLAYING TREBLE G

In this level we will not be playing most of our ledger line flashcard notes. There is an except to this and that is the treble G note.

If you remember the note F for **F**udge is the F above treble C.

The G note right above that F is the note that will be in this weeks lesson and subsequent weeks lessons as well.

Have your child locate this G on the piano in the correct location so they are familiar with it before they begin their practice song.

TEACHING THE PRACTICE SONG:

This song has both hands start in C position. However in measure 3 the left hand crosses over the right hand to play a treble C with its 2 finger. After it plays the treble C is should go back. However it isn't going back to its original position. It is moving to place its 1 finger on middle C. Then in measure 7 have the left hand cross over the right hand to play the treble F with its 2 finger. After it plays the F it returns back to its normal C position location

Once your child masters the song have them add in the pedal which starts on the first note and doesn't lift until beat 3 of the last measure. Make sure their heel is on the floor the whole time.

Make sure to have your child write in the counts for this song and count it aloud with clapping before attempting to play it. Point out to your child that we are in 3/4 time.

Daily Practice Log (4-6 days @ 15-20 minutes each day):

❋ *Flashcards for terms*

❋ *Flashcards for all notes (find the location on the piano for some of them)*

❋ *Practice song*

❋ *Corresponding Theory Chapter*

❋ *Hands together C & G Scale going up and down*

❋ *Flashcards all treble clef ledger lines combined*

❋ *Flashcard bass clef ledger line notes combined*

❋ *Play C & F & G major chord*

PRACTICE SONG lesson 6: Summer Sky

Summer Sky

ANSWERS FOR PARENTS

Summer Sky

Practice song answer for parents... Don't let your child see this answer at any time:

CHAPTER 4: More Major Chords and Playing 8va

LESSON 1

PLAYING A FERMATA

You added to the flashcards in a previous lesson the term fermata, so your child should be familiar by now with its concept. We will be applying the fermata to our song this week.

The very last note of this weeks lesson song has a fermata over both the right hand and the left hand notes. That means that both hands hold those notes extra time than they are supposed to.

The notes that have a fermata are a half note and would normally receive 2 beats and would be counted 2-3 (because they start on beat 2). Tell your child to count the normal 2-3 but than say the words "hold extra long" after they say 2-3. That will give them a general idea of what the fermata should feel like.

This method can apply any time your child sees a fermata. Have them count the beats like normal and then say the words "hold extra long."

8va

The next term we will add to our flashcards is 8va. 8va stands for playing the note you see written either an octave higher or lower than written. If the 8va is written above the note, we play one octave higher and if the 8va is written below the note we play one octave lower.

For example, if we we saw a treble C with an 8va above it we would play that treble C one octave higher. Another way to say that would be we would play the C ABOVE treble C. That is what one octave higher means.

An example of playing one octave lower would be to imagine a song has a bass C (the normal LH C position). If we saw an 8va written below that bass C we would play the C BELOW bass c in place of the actual bass C.

8va is not to be confused with one hand crossing over the other. If it says 8va it means to play it with the normal hand...just higher or lower.

8va−−−⌐

On the front of the flashcard draw the image to the right. On the back write 8va - means to play one octave higher or lower.

TEACHING THE PRACTICE SONG:

This song has the right hand with the 1 finger on treble C for the whole song. The left hand is in C position the whole song.

The pattern to show your child in this song is it goes from single notes playing 4ths, then 3rds, then 2nds then 5ths. That sequence is then repeated by the left hand. Then it returns to the RH and does the same intervals (4ths, 3rds, 2nds, 5ths) but now as 2 notes played at once. The the LH follows that same pattern.

Measure 17-20 has contrary motion in each hand. Practice the whole song hands apart and master it hands separate before attempting hands together. Especially focus your hands apart practice on measure 17-20.

When starting hands together on measure 17-20 take it one measure at a time. Play measure 17 hands apart, then together. Then play measure 18 hands apart then together. Then play just measures 17-18 hands together before doing the same practice method on measure 19 and so on. This is the method that should be used with all challenging material.

Daily Practice Log (4-6 days @ 15-20 minutes each day):
- ❋ *Flashcards for terms*
- ❋ *Flashcards for all notes (find the location on the piano)*
- ❋ *Practice song*
- ❋ *Corresponding Theory Chapter*
- ❋ *Hands together C & G Scale going up and down*
- ❋ *Flashcards all treble clef ledger lines combined*
- ❋ *Flashcard bass clef ledger line notes combined*
- ❋ *Play C & F & G major chord*

PRACTICE SONG lesson 1: Carousel

carousel

ANSWERS FOR PARENTS

carousel

Practice song answer for parents... Don't let your child see this answer at any time:

LESSON 2

LEARNING MAJOR CHORDS - D MAJOR

Your child has learned the chords C, F, and G. Those 3 chords use only the white notes. For now practice those 3 chords together as a group.

We will now learn a new group of 3 chords and this group all has 1 black note in the middle.

The first note that is played in any chord is the letter name of the chord. We are learning about the D major chord which means our first note will be a D.

Using the skip method gets a little tricky with this group of 3 chords. Let me show you why. The next note that is played is a skip above the first note. Since our first note is D, a skip above D is an F#. Not a plain old regular F. Well, why is it F# and not F? The reason is clear in the alternative method.

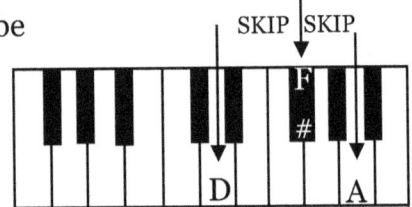

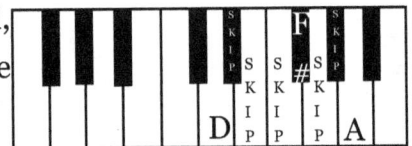

Major chords must always skip 3 notes then skip 2 notes. Skipping three notes after the D note lands us on F#, not F. That is the why behind the chord. From the F# we have to skip 2 more notes to find the last note of the chord as note A.

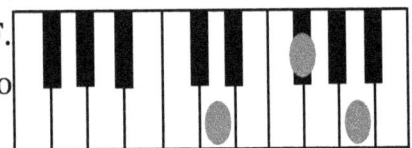

Have your child play a D, F# AND A notes all at the same time in their RIGHT hand. Make sure they use the 1 - 3 - 5 fingers when doing this. This is a D chord and is demonstrated in the image to the right.

Remember, its not a chord unless all the notes are played at the exact same time.
They should be familiar with where a F# is from their theory, but if they forgot, a F# is the black note directly above/after the regular F white note.

Playing 8va IN THE RIGHT HAND

You learned what 8va meant in the previous lesson. In this lesson, your child's song will have the first 8va in their music. It is on the very last note of the song. It is ABOVE the treble clef note which means we need to play that note but one octave HIGHER. The note is treble C (the c above middle C), so the 8va means to play a C one higher than treble C.

TEACHING THE PRACTICE SONG:

This song has both hands on C position for the whole song except for the very last 8va note in the RH and when the LH cross over note in measure 8.

The left hand crossing over happens in the second line at measure 8. Here the left hand crosses over the right so that the LEFT hand plays ALL 3 treble C notes in that measure. After measure 8 the left hand immediately goes back to its C position.

A challenge with learning a song the child may be familiar with is they may try to play it the way they hear it in their head and not the way it is written in the music. For this reason, make sure they write their counts in and that they count the song aloud even though the rhythm of the song is fairly straightforward.

Make sure the last note of the song is played one octave higher than treble C because of the 8va.

Daily Practice Log (4-6 days @ 15-20 minutes each day):
* *Flashcards for all notes (find the location on the piano)*
* *Practice song*
* *Corresponding Theory Chapter*
* *Hands together C & G Scale going up and down*
* *Flashcards all treble clef ledger lines combined*
* *Flashcard bass clef ledger line notes combined*
* *Play C & F & G major chord*
* *Play D major chord (Do not do at the same time as C,F, G chords)*

PRACTICE SONG lesson 2: Row, Row, Row Your Boat

Row, Row, Row Your Boat

Row, Row, Row Your Boat

Practice song answer for parents... Don't let your child see this answer at any time:

LESSON 3

PLAYING 8va IN THE LEFT HAND

In the previous lesson, you learned that 8va in the RH means to go one octave higher. If you see a 8va in the LH it means the opposite. It means to play the note one octave LOWER. In this lesson your child will have their first 8va in their left hand. It is on the very last note of the song. It is BELOW the bass clef note which means we need to play that note, but one octave LOWER than its written. The note written is the E right above bass C so the 8va means to play an E one lower than that spot.

Notice that not only does that note play 8va, but it also has a fermata above it. So that means you need to make sure your child holds that note counting, "1-2-3" and then say "hold extra time."

TEACHING THE PRACTICE SONG:

The right hand is on the B directly below treble C and is played with the 1 finger. Point out to your child where it skips and where it steps and also the very long tie in the RH. Point out to your child that the tie holds over the line and continues onto the next line.

The LH is on the B directly below middle C and is played with the 1 finger. The LH also has a lot of steps and skips that you should scout out with your child before they begin playing it.

Notice the pedal marking and that it starts on the very first note and does not let up until after the fermata of the last note is finished. Make sure your Child's heel never leaves the floor while they play this.

Make sure to have your child write in the counts for this song and count it aloud with clapping before attempting to play it. Point out to your child that we are in 3/4 time. Make sure they hold out their dotted half notes the full 3 counts.

Daily Practice Log (4-6 days @ 15-20 minutes each day):
- ❀ *Flashcards for terms*
- ❀ *Flashcards for all notes (find the location on the piano)*
- ❀ *Practice song*
- ❀ *Corresponding Theory Chapter*
- ❀ *Hands together C & G Scale going up and down*
- ❀ *Flashcards all treble clef ledger lines combined*
- ❀ *Flashcard bass clef ledger line notes combined*
- ❀ *Play C & F & G major chord*
- ❀ *Play D major chord (Not at the same time as C,F,G)*

PRACTICE SONG lesson 3: Setting Sun

Setting Sun

Stephanie Parker

Setting Sun

LESSON 4

LEARNING MAJOR CHORDS - E MAJOR

Your child learned the 1st of 3 chords that has a black note in the middle. We will now add the next chord like that...The E major chord.

The first note that is played in any chord is the letter name of the chord. We are learning about the E major chord which means our first note will be an E.

As explained with the D Chord, the skip method gets a little confusing with the group of chords that have a black note in the middle.   For that reason, there won't be an explanation of the skip method from this point on. However, the image on the right with the skip method will still remain.

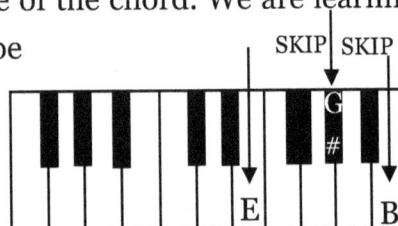

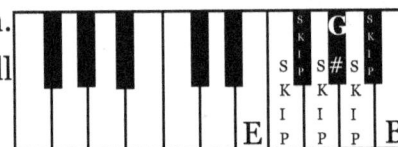

Remind your child that major chords must always skip 3 notes then skip 2 notes. Skipping three notes after the E note lands us on G#, not G. From the G# we have to skip 2 more notes to find the last note of the chord as note B.

E MAJOR CHORD

Have your child play a E, G# AND B note all at the same time in their RIGHT hand. Make sure they use the 1 - 3 - 5 fingers when doing this. This is an E chord and is demonstrated in the image to the right.

Remember, it's not a chord unless all the notes are played at the exact same time.

They should be familiar with where a G# is from their theory, but if they forgot a G# is the black note directly above/after the regular G white note.

PLAYING 8va IN BOTH HANDS

If you look in this weeks practice song, you will see that the last note has an 8va above the RH and below the LH at the same time. When you see this occur, the RH goes up an octave and the LH goes down an octave. In this example, the RH will play the C above treble C and the LH will play the C below bass C. Both hands will play those notes simultaneously as in this example they both occur on beat 1.

TEACHING THE PRACTICE SONG:

This song has both the RH beginning with the 1 finger on treble C and the LH with the 5 finger on bass C.

Point out to your child that the RH steps up all the way to treble G. Point out to your child the ties in the song and remind them that any tied notes hold. Notice in measure 11 the Right hand plays on beat 1 and then ties (holds) until the end of the next measure. During this time the LH enters on beat 2 and plays. That is a tricky rhythm, so have them be extra careful with this section and spend time here especially clapping it out after they write in the counts for the whole song.

Daily Practice Log (4-6 days @ 15-20 minutes each day):
- ❀ *Flashcards for terms*
- ❀ *Flashcards for all notes (find the location on the piano)*
- ❀ *Practice song*
- ❀ *Corresponding Theory Chapter*
- ❀ *Hands together C & G Scale going up and down*
- ❀ *Flashcards all treble clef ledger lines combined*
- ❀ *Flashcard bass clef ledger line notes combined*
- ❀ *Play C & F & G major chord*
- ❀ *Play D & E major chord (Not at the same time as C,F,G)*

PRACTICE SONG lesson 4: Daydream

Daydream

Stephanie Parker

ANSWERS FOR PARENTS

Daydream

Practice song answer for parents... Don't let your child see this answer at any time:

Daily Practice Log (4-6 days @ 15-20 minutes each day):
- ❋ _Flashcards for terms_
- ❋ _Flashcards for all notes (find the location on the piano)_
- ❋ _Practice song_
- ❋ _Corresponding Theory Chapter_
- ❋ _Hands together C & G Scale going up and down_
- ❋ _Flashcards all treble clef ledger lines combined_
- ❋ _Flashcard bass clef ledger line notes combined_
- ❋ _Play C & F & G major chord_
- ❋ _Play D & E & A major chord (Not at the same time as C,F,G)_

LESSON 5

LEARNING MAJOR CHORDS - A MAJOR

Your child learned 2 of the 3 chords that has a black note in the middle. We will now add the last chord like that...The A major chord.

The first note that is played in any chord is the letter name of the chord. We are learning about the A major chord which means our first note will be an A.

Remind your child that major chords must always skip 3 notes then skip 2 notes. Skipping three notes after the A note lands us on C#, not C. From the C# we have to skip 2 more notes to find the last note of the chord as note E.

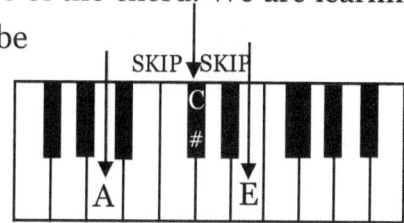

Have your child play a A, C# AND E note all at the same time in their RIGHT hand. Make sure they use the 1 - 3 - 5 fingers when doing this. This is an A chord and is demonstrated in the images to the right.

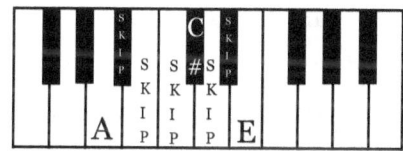

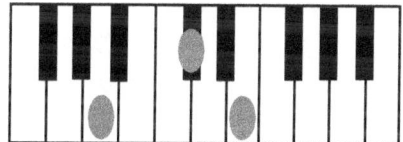

Remember, it's not a chord unless all the notes are played at the exact same time.

They should be familiar with where a C# is from their theory, but if they forgot a C# is the black note directly above/after the regular C white note.

At this point, keep separate the C, F, G chords from D, E, A chords. First practice C,F.G then do something else. Possibly scales or flashcards would be a good choice. Then do the D, E, A chords.

You want to keep the group of chords that use only the white notes separate from the chords that have a black note in the middle for now.

TEACHING THE PRACTICE SONG:

The LH is in C position and doesn't move the whole song until the very last note when it has an 8va and needs to go to the C below bass C. The rhythm in the LH is quarter note - rest - quarter note - rest almost the whole song. Have your child clap just the LH before attempting to play it. It should sound like 1 - shh - 3 - shh - 1 - shh - 3 - shh and so on.

The RH should be counted aloud and clapped after you finish hearing your child clap the LH. The half notes in the right hand while the left hand does quarter note/rest pattern can be tricky. Make sure your child holds the half note for 2 full beats while the left hand is having a rest. Also make sure you can hear when both hands have a rest at the same time (like in measure 3).

Just like last lessons practice song, the last measure has both hands playing 8va. However this time it is not at the same time. Make sure the LH playing an octave lower happens on beat 1 and the RH playing an octave higher happens on beat 3.

Make sure to have your child write in the counts for this song and count it aloud while playing.

PRACTICE SONG lesson 5: Dizzy

Dizzy

ANSWERS FOR PARENTS

Dizzy

Practice song answer for parents... Don't let your child see this answer at any time:

CHAPTER 5: Playing Sharps & Flats

LESSON 1

D MAJOR SCALE RIGHT HAND GOING UP

Your child has learned the C and G scale and can play them hands together going up and down. The next scale we will learn is the D scale. The D scale uses the exact same fingering as the C and the G scale.

The D scale has 2 black notes: the F# and C#. So, instead of playing a white note on F and on C you will need to play the black note right above those notes.

The C scale had 0 black notes, the G scale had 1 black note - F#, and the D scale will have 2 black notes - F# and C#. Make sure your child can verbally articulate this. Ask them before they play each of their scales these two questions:

> 1) How many black notes are in this scale?
> 2) What are they?

The image to the right shows what the D major scale looks like on the piano and which notes are played in the D scale.

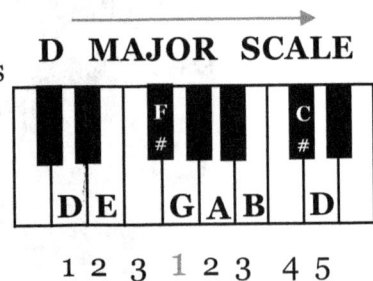

This week have your child play the right hand D scale going up only. Below are the notes and fingering for this scale in the Right hand going up. The large number is where the thumb tunnels under the 3.

D MAJOR SCALE

D E G A B D
1 2 3 1 2 3 4 5

D - E - F# - G - A - B - C# - D

1   2   3   1   2   3   4   5

Note that the 3 plays the F# and the tunnel happens AFTER the F#.

HALF STEPS

The concept of half step has been discussed in relation to the major chords. Your child learned that to find the 2nd note of any major chord they have to skip 3 half steps. Now teach your child more what the term half step means.

HALF STEP UP FROM D

A half step is moving to the very next closest note either up or down. This means, make sure you are including black and white notes when looking for the very next closest note as demonstrated by the image to the right.

HALF STEP DOWN FROM D

PLAYING SHARPS IN THE RIGHT HAND

You have taught your child to play sharps for a while now in their scales where they played the black note instead of the white note. Now
it is time to show them how to recognize that in their music and play it in their practice songs.

When your child sees a sharp in their music it simply means to move one half step to the right or up the piano.

When their hand is in position for their song, it should be resting so that each white note gets one finger on it. Fingers should not be squished with multiple fingers on one note, nor should they be spread out so that fingers are skipping over notes.

Let's say your child's right hand is in C position. This would mean their 1 finger would be on middle C, 2 finger on D, 3 finger on E, 4 finger on F, and 5 finger on G. Have them put their hand on the piano like that now and show them how each note gets one finger. Then have them play the example to the right.

Now, lets say the music has an F# in it instead of a regular F note. The hand should not move. The 4 finger that would have played the F note simply moves up now to play the F#. Whatever finger is "assigned" to the white note is also assigned to its sharp.

Have them play the example to the right starting with their 1 finger in C position. Make sure they use their 4 finger to play the F#.

Make sure your child applies this finger number rule when playing sharps in their practice songs.

HOW SHARPS WORK WITHIN A MEASURE

When a note is sharped, all of the same exact notes in that measure are sharped too. The sharp does not need to be written in. It is an understood rule. Once you reach the bar line at the end of the measure, the sharp that was in the previous measure gets erased. Think of the bar line as a big eraser line. All the notes following the bar line no longer have the sharp associated with it.

The example below demonstrates this principle. The first note has a F# which makes all the rest of the notes in that measure turn into F# as well. Then comes a bar line (eraser line) so the second measure the F# is gone and all the notes are the regular F note. Have your child play this example below. You should hear them play

F#-F#-F#-F# / F-F-F-F

TEACHING THE PRACTICE SONG:

The RH 5 finger is on the E above treble C. Use the 4 finger to play the D# right below it. Remember that a # only lasts until the bar line (the eraser line) and then in the next measure it should be played on the white note if no sharp is written in. So in measure 2 and 7 it is a regular D not a D#.

The LH position has the 1 finger on middle C for the whole song.
In measure 1 and 6 there is an D# at the beginning of the measure followed by an additional D notes later in the measure. Remember the sharp rule in those measures. The D stays sharp for those whole measures so on beat 4 of those measures make sure it is still a D# your child is playing.

On measures 2 and 7 (the measure following the D#) is another D. Remember the D note in measures 2 and 7 follows the bar line (eraser line) which mean the D is no longer sharp. Make sure your child plays the regular D note in those measures.

This is an arrangement of a famous piece by Beethoven. It is not the actual song. This can make learning a song fun, yet challenging. That is because when a song is already familiar to a student it is easy for them to play it the way they hear it in their head and not the way it is written in the music. So, make sure your child writes in the counts and counts aloud through the whole song so it is played just like it is written.

Daily Practice Log (4-6 days @ 15-20 minutes each day):

- ✳ *Flashcards for all notes (find the location on the piano)*
- ✳ *Practice song*
- ✳ *Corresponding Theory Chapter*
- ✳ *Hands together C & G Scale going up and down*
- ✳ *Flashcards all treble clef ledger lines combined*
- ✳ *Flashcard bass clef ledger line notes combined*
- ✳ *Play C & F & G major chord*
- ✳ *Play D & E & A major chord (Not at the same time as C,F,G)*
- ✳ *Play the D scale RH going up*

PRACTICE SONG lesson 1: Fur Elise

Fur Elise

Stephanie Parker

ANSWERS FOR PARENTS

Fur Elise

Practice song answer for parents... Don't let your child see this answer at any time

LESSON 2

D MAJOR SCALE RH UP AND DOWN

D MAJOR SCALE RH

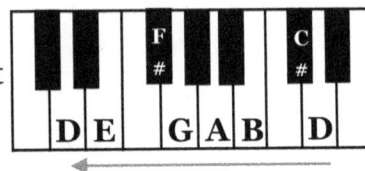

To learn the scale heading in the downward direction first have your child go up the scale and hold the D at the top. Then have them go back down.

The finger pattering for going down the scale is the exact same finger pattern for the C & G scale heading down. (5-4-3-2-1-3-2-1)

Notice once the 1 finger lands on the G that the the 3 finger will be hopping over the 1 finger. When it hops over on this scale it lands on the F# which is a black note. This will feel different at first to your child, so go over with them to expect this.

Below are the notes and fingering for this scale in the Right hand going up and down. Going up, the large number is where the 1 tunnels under the 3. Going down, the large number is where the 3 bunny hops over the 1.

Once that makes sense to your child have your child practice independently going up and down the G scale.

D MAJOR SCALE RH

GOING UP   D-E-F#-G-A-B-C#-D

             1 2 3 1 2 3 4 5

1 2 3 1 2 3 4 5

D MAJOR SCALE RH

GOING DOWN   D-C#-B-A-G-F#-E-D

             5 4 3 2 1 3 2 1

120

PLAYING A SHARP IN THE LH

The same rules for playing a sharp in the right hand apply to playing it in the left hand. Make sure their fingers are not be squished with multiple fingers on one note, nor are they spread out so that fingers are skipping over notes.

Lets say your child's left hand is in C position. This would mean their 5 finger would be on bass C, 4 finger on D, 3 finger on E, 2 finger on F, and 1 finger on G. Have them put their hand on the piano like that now and show them how each note gets one finger. Then have them play the example to the right.

Now lets say the music has an F# in it instead of a regular F note. The hand should not move. The 2 finger that would have played the F note simply moves up now to play the F#. Whatever finger is "assigned" to the white note is also assigned to its sharp.

Have them play the example to the right starting with their 5 finger in C position. Make sure they use their 2 finger to play the F#.

Make sure your child apply this finger number rule when playing sharps in their practice songs.

TEACHING THE PRACTICE SONG:

The RH has the 1 finger on the D above middle C for the whole song. Make sure that anytime an F# is played the 3 finger is used on it.

The LH has a 3 finger on the F# below the middle C for the whole song until the very last note when it crosses over the right hand to play the D above treble C.

Learn the right hand first with counting it aloud and then learn the left hand. Once both hands are mastered hands apart, then begin learning it hands together.

In measure 1,7,9, and 11 there is an F# at the beginning of the measure followed by 2 more F notes. Remember the sharp rule in those measures. The F stays sharp for those whole measures so on beat 2 and 3 of those measures make sure it is still a F# your child is playing.

Make sure to have your child write in the counts for this song and count it aloud while playing playing close attention to the rests at the end of some of the measures.

Daily Practice Log (4-6 days @ 15-20 minutes each day):
- ✳ *Flashcards for terms*
- ✳ *Flashcards for all notes (find the location on the piano)*
- ✳ *Practice song*
- ✳ *Corresponding Theory Chapter*
- ✳ *Hands together C & G Scale going up and down*
- ✳ *Flashcards all treble clef ledger lines combined*
- ✳ *Flashcard bass clef ledger line notes combined*
- ✳ *Play C & F & G major chord*
- ✳ *Play D & E & A major chord (Not at the same time as C,F,G)*
- ✳ *Play the D scale RH going up*

Stephanie Parker

PRACTICE SONG lesson 2: The Waterfall

The Waterfall

The Waterfall

Practice song answer for parents... Don't let your child see this answer at any time:

LESSON 3

D MAJOR SCALE LEFT HAND GOING UP

D MAJOR SCALE LH

The left hand D scale follows the same pattern as the LH C & G scale. That means your fingering going up will be 5-4-3-2-1-3-2-1.

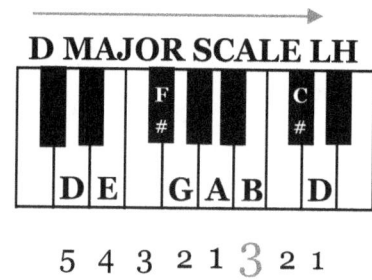

5 4 3 2 1 3 2 1

Below are the notes and fingering for this scale in the left hand going up. The large number is where the 3 bunny hops over the 1.

D-E-F#-G-A-B-C#-D

5 4 3 2 1 3 2 1

SKIP SKIP

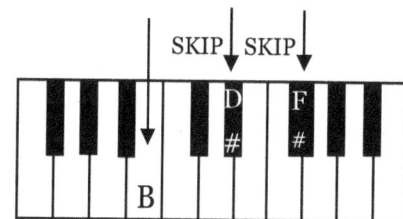

LEARNING MAJOR CHORDS - B MAJOR

This chord is different because it has TWO black notes.

The first note that is played in any chord is the letter name of the chord. We are learning about the B major chord which means our first note will be a B. That is our last regular note.

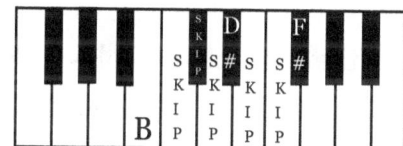

B MAJOR CHORD

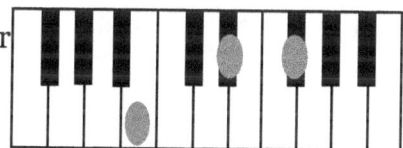

Remind your child that major chords must always skip 3 notes then skip 2 notes. Skipping three notes after the B note lands us on D#, not D. From the D# we have to skip 2 more notes to find the last note of the chord as note F#.

Have your child play a B, D# AND F# note all at the same time in their RIGHT hand. Make sure they use the 1 - 3 - 5 fingers when doing this. This is an B chord and is demonstrated in the images to the right.

Remember, its not a chord unless all the notes are played at the exact same time.

HOW TO PRACTICE THE MAJOR CHORDS

The B major chord is the trickiest and the last of the major chords we will be learning in this level.

For this reason, practice this one alone and separate from the other 2 groups of major chords. I have my students practice C,F, and G major chord. Then I have them practice the D,E,A major chord. Lastly, I have them play the B major chord.

The goal is for you to only have to say, "Play C,F & G major chord. Now play D,E & A major chord. Last play the B major chord."

If those instructions confuses them, you can preface the C,F and G chords by saying the all white note chords. You can preface the D,E,A chords by saying the chords with a black note in the middle. You can preface the B major chord by saying the tricky chord.

The goal is to get away from those memory device tricks as quickly as possible and just have them be able to play C,F,G // D,E,A // B major chord by simply saying play the C,F,G chord. Now play the D,E,A chord. Last play the B chord.

The practice log from this point out will have the chord homework listed as C,F,G // D,E,A // B major chords. Make sure to separate them and use the practice methods listed above.

TEACHING THE PRACTICE SONG:

The LH is in C position the whole song. It has a repeating pattern where the C plays followed by the E and G notes played simultaneously.

The RH is in the C position the whole song as well. The 4th finger that would normally play F instead now plays the F# in the song.

Make sure the slurs in measure 5 and 6 are played legato and the rest of the songs staccatos are played short and detached. Don't let the staccatos speed up their playing. Make sure their counts stay slow and steady through the whole song.

Write in the counts nice and big. Learn it hands apart first and then play hands together paying close attention to the rests making sure that the notes in the RH and LH that are on top of each other are played at the same time.

Daily Practice Log (4-6 days @ 15-20 minutes each day):

- ❋ *Flashcards for terms*
- ❋ *Flashcards for all notes (find the location on the piano)*
- ❋ *Practice song*
- ❋ *Corresponding Theory Chapter*
- ❋ *Hands together C & G Scale going up and down*
- ❋ *Flashcards all treble clef ledger lines combined*
- ❋ *Flashcard bass clef ledger line notes combined*
- ❋ *Play C & F & G major chord*
- ❋ *Play D & E & A major chord (Not at the same time as C,F,G)*
- ❋ *Play the D scale RH going up and down*

PRACTICE SONG lesson 3: Funhouse

Funhouse

ANSWERS FOR PARENTS

Funhouse

Practice song answer for parents... Don't let your child see this answer at any time:

LESSON 4

D MAJOR SCALE LEFT HAND UP AND DOWN

To learn the scale heading in the downward direction in the left hand first have your child go up the scale and hold the D at the top, then have them go back down.

The finger pattering for the LH going down the scale is the exact same finger patter for the LH C & G scale heading down. 1-2-3-1-2-3-4-5

Below are the notes and fingering for this scale in the left hand going down. The large number is where the 1 finger tunnels under the 3 finger.

D-C#-B-A-G-F#-E-D

1 2 3 1 2 3 4 5

Once that makes sense to your child have your child practice independently going up and down the D scale in the left hand.

GOING UP   D-E-F#-G-A-B-C#-D

5 4 3 2 1 3 2 1

GOING DOWN   D-C#-B-A-G-F#-E-D

1 2 3 1 2 3 4 5

PLAYING A FLAT IN THE RIGHT HAND

Your child has been identifying flats in their theory, but they have never played one up until this point.

When your child sees a flat in their music it simply means to move one half step to the left or down the piano.

Lets say your child's right hand is in C position. This would mean their 1 finger would be on middle C, 2 finger on D, 3 finger on E, 4 finger on F, and 5 finger on G. Have them put their hand on the piano like that now and show them how each note gets one finger. Then have them play the example to the right.

Now lets say the music has an E ♭ in it instead of a regular E note. The hand should not move. The 3 finger that would have played the E note simply moves down now to play the E . Whatever finger is "assigned" to the white note is also assigned to its flat.

Have them play the example to the right starting with their 1 finger in C position. Make sure they use their 3 finger to play the E ♭ .

This can feel a little odd to a new student as the fingers feel a little more stretched out than they are used to. Make sure to play close attention that they are using the correct finger numbers for this reason.

Make sure your child applies this finger number rule when playing flats in their practice songs.

HOW FLATS WORK WITHIN A MEASURE

When a note is flatted, all of the same exact notes in that measure are flatted too. The additional flats do not need to be written in. It is a understood rule. Once you reach the bar line at the end of the measure the flat that was in the previous measure gets erased. Think of the bar line as a big eraser line. All the notes following the bar line no longer have the flat associated with it.

The example below demonstrates this principle. The first note has a E-flat which makes all the rest of the notes in that measure turn into E-flats as well. Then comes a bar line (eraser line) so in the second measure the E-flat is gone and all the notes are the regular E note. Have your child play this example below. You should hear them play:

E♭ - E♭ - E♭ - E♭ / E - E - E - E

TEACHING THE PRACTICE SONG:

The LH has the 5 finger on the F below middle C. It stays there the whole song until the very last note when it moves down and plays a bass C with the 5 finger. Watch for a curved pinky finger.

The RH should have the 3 finger on the A-flat above middle C.

Make sure to have your child write in the counts for this song and count it aloud while playing. Have them play careful attention to beat 1 in each measure where the LH plays and the RH is silent until the RH plays on beat 2.

Daily Practice Log (4-6 days @ 15-20 minutes each day):
* *Flashcards for terms*
* *Flashcards for all notes (find the location on the piano)*
* *Practice song*
* *Corresponding Theory Chapter*
* *Hands together C & G Scale going up and down*
* *Flashcards all treble clef ledger lines combined*
* *Flashcard bass clef ledger line notes combined*
* *Play C, F, G // D, E, A // B major chord*
* *Play the D scale RH going up and down*
* *Play the D scale LH going up*

Stephanie Parker

PRACTICE SONG lesson 4: A Sad Story

A Sad Story

Hand Shift

ANSWERS FOR PARENTS

A Sad Story

Practice song answer for parents... Don't let your child see this answer at any time:

LESSON 5

D MAJOR SCALE HANDS TOGETHER UP

You have taught your child to play the D scale hands apart. If they still struggle hands apart, really focus on the scale practice so they can master it and move on to this step of playing the D scale in both hands at the same time.

Before beginning, remind your child that even though they're starting on D, it will be the exact same fingering as the C & G scale.

Also remind your child that, when playing a scale hands together, both of the hands do the exact same thing, but in reverse of each other. So, going up the scale, the right hand will be tunneling under the 3 finger and the left hand will have the 3rd finger hopping over.

Here is what that will look like:

$$D - E - F\# - G - A - B - C\# - D$$

RIGHT HAND: 1 2   3   1   2   3   4   5

LEFT HAND: 5   4   3   2   1   3   2   1

Notice that the "tunnel" and the "bunny hop" do not happen at the exact same time. First comes the tunnel followed two notes later by the bunny hop.

When teaching this to your child take it slow. Have them play just the D's together. Once they do that with ease, then have them play D's to E's together. Once that happens have them do the first 3 notes together.

On the 3rd note, F#, make sure your child plays the F# and not the F white note.

This is where it'll get harder. While both hands are on the F# note, have them just hold the note down and really talk through what will happen next. Next the left hand will play the 2 finger on the G, but the right hand will have the thumb tunnel under to the G.

When they master playing the G's together, pause. Make sure they shifted their whole right hand in line with the new thumb position. If everything looks right, move on to the A's together which is pretty simple.

Here comes the bunny hop. While holding the A's down in both hands, have the LH 3 finger bunny hop over the thumb. Once it's in position to play the B have both hands play the B's together simultaneously. Then, shift the left hand to be in line with the new position of the third finger.

The rest is not to difficult as your Child's hand is in position and ready to play the C#'s together and then the D's together. Just make sure they play C# and not the C white note.

Stop here. Don't try and go down the scale yet. Do this a couple more times throughout the lesson until you're sure you child will be able to practice it during the week.

At this stage, do not have your child go straight to hands together practice each day with the D scale. Have them play the right hand scale up and down, then the left hand scale up and down. Then have them do hands together going up only.

PLAYING A FLAT IN THE LEFT HAND

The same rules for playing a flat in the right hand apply to playing it in the left hand. Make sure their fingers are not squished with multiple fingers on one note, nor are they spread out so that fingers are skipping over notes.

Lets say your child's left hand is in C position. This would mean their 5 finger would be on bass C, 4 finger on D, 3 finger on E, 2 finger on F, and 1 finger on G. Have them put their hand on the piano like that now and show them how each note gets one finger. Then have them play the example to the right.

Now lets say the music has an E♭ in it instead of a regular E note. The hand should not move. The 3 finger that would have played the E note simply moves down now to play the E♭. Whatever finger is "assigned" to the white note is also assigned to its flat.

Have them play the example to the right starting with their 5 finger in LH C position. Make sure they use their 3 finger to play the E ♭ .

Make sure your child applies this finger number rule when playing flats in their practice songs.

TEACHING THE PRACTICE SONG:

The LH is in C position and doesn't move the whole song. It plays the same 4 notes over and over again. So get your child very comfortable with playing their left hand alone. Make sure all their fingers are curved as they play those 4 notes over and over.

The right hand is in the C position the whole song as well. The middle C note doesn't change. It is the top note that you will notice that is stepping down. It starts as intervals of a 5th, then 4th, then 3rd (Played with a flat) then a 2nd. That pattern is repeated the whole song. Practice the RH alone as well and have your child get very comfortable with it before attempting to put the two hands together.

In measure 3, 7 and 17 the middle C is on the bottom while the E-flat plays simultaneously above it. Keep in mind the flat rule in those measures. The E stays flat for those whole measures so on beat 3 of those measures make sure it is still an E-flat your child is playing.

Write in the counts for the song because the rhythm is very challenging in this song, so during the hand alone practice make sure your child is counting everything. Then make sure they count as well when putting it hands together.

Daily Practice Log (4-6 days @ 15-20 minutes each day):

* Flashcards for terms
* Flashcards for all notes (find the location on the piano)
* Practice song
* Corresponding Theory Chapter
* Hands together C & G Scale going up and down
* Flashcards all treble clef ledger lines combined
* Flashcard bass clef ledger line notes combined
* Play C, F, G // D, E, A // B major chord
* Play the D scale RH going up and down
* Play the D scale LH going up and down
* Play the D scale Hands together going up

Stephanie Parker

PRACTICE SONG lesson 5: Walking Bass

Walking Bass

Walking Bass

Practice song answer for parents... Don't let your child see this answer at any time:

LESSON 6

D MAJOR SCALE HANDS TOGETHER UP AND DOWN

If your child is able to go up the D scale hands together, then move on to teaching them this week about coming back down the scale. If going up the scale hands together is still a challenge for them, give them another week or two just going up hands together and then at that time return to this part of lesson 6.

Just like when they went up the scale the two hands did the opposite of one another (one tunneled and the other one bunny hopped), the same thing will happen going down except the two hands will switch which one they're doing.

On the way down, the right hand will bunny hop when it runs out of fingers and the left hand will tunnel under after the 3 finger.

The best way to teach going down the scale is to have them go up the scale hands together and stop when they get to the top on that D and rest there. Now you will talk them through each note.

For the first two notes, their fingers are exactly where they should be just don't forget the C#. So have them go down playing the C#'s together then the B's together and then have them pause holding down the B's.

On the B, the left hand is on the 3 finger, so it will need to have the 1 finger (thumb) tunnel under to the A. Once its in position, have BOTH hands play the A's at the same time and then shift the left hand to be in position with the new thumb location.

G's together is next and is fairly simple, but it means the right hand has run out of fingers. This means the right hand now needs to have the 3rd finger bunny hop over the thumb and get into position to play the F# (Make sure both hands are ready to play the F# and not the white note F). Once it's in position have the two hands play the F#'s at the same time. Then have the right hand shift the hand so its in position with the new location of the 3rd finger.

The last two notes are all lined up and ready to go, so have them play the E's then the D's together.

If your child catches on to this concept fairly quickly, they can go straight to hands together D scale in their practice time. If it is a bit of a struggle still, then have their scale practice time be:

1)RH hands apart D scale up and down

2) LH hands apart D scale up and down

3) Hands together D scale up and down.

PLAYING MIDDLE D IN THE LEFT HAND

You have taught your child to play the ledger line flashcard G (right about the note F - Fudge) in the right hand. Now, we learn to play one of the left hand ledger line notes.

D - located directly above middle C played with the LH

Your child should be familiar that the note in the image to the right is a D from their flashcard practice. The location of that D on the piano is right above middle C.

Show your child the images below. Point out how middle C is on the first ledger line above the bass clef staff and the D is on the space directly above that middle C. That means that the note it is telling you to play is the note directly above middle C which is a D directly above middle C.

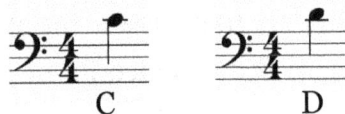

C   D

TEACHING THE PRACTICE SONG:

This weeks practice song has the middle D discussed in the teaching above. Notice the finger numbers in the left hand says 5 finger on G. That is the G directly below middle C. If you place your 5 finger on that G, your 1 finger in your left hand naturally falls on the D above middle C. Any time you see a note that looks like the image to the right you will play the middle D that your LH 1 finger is on.

In measures 9 & 10 the left hand crosses over the right hand to play the E-flat. The following notes (D-C-G) in that measure are played by the RH. The LH only plays the E-flat. After measure 10 the left hand needs to go back to its original position with a 2 finger on middle C.

The right hand has a 1 finger on G and that position does not change the whole song. Make sure the B your child plays is flat. Notice that the B-flat in measure 4 (and the other measures like it) has a line note to a line note. That means it's a skip from the B-flat up to the D. Remember a skip always skips 1 full letter, in this case it skips over the letter/note C.

Ask your child to identify the pedal markings in this song. Have them show you where the pedal begins and ends (it starts in measure 1 and ends in measure 8. then it begins again at measure 13 and ends after counting 1-2-3-4 on the last note of the song). Don't add pedal until all their notes and rhythms can be played correctly. It is the last step.

Make sure to write in all the counts. There are a lot of rests make sure as your child counts aloud that they observe the rests.

Daily Practice Log (4-6 days @ 15-20 minutes each day):
- ❋ *Flashcards for terms*
- ❋ *Flashcards for all notes (find the location on the piano)*
- ❋ *Practice song*
- ❋ *Corresponding Theory Chapter*
- ❋ *Hands together C & G Scale going up and down*
- ❋ *Flashcards all treble clef ledger lines combined*
- ❋ *Flashcard bass clef ledger line notes combined*
- ❋ *Play C, F, G //D, E, A // B major chord*
- ❋ *Play the D scale RH going up and down*
- ❋ *Play the D scale LH going up and down*
- ❋ *Play the D Scale hands together going up and down.*

PRACTICE SONG lesson 6: Mysterious Morning

Mysterious Morning

ANSWERS FOR PARENTS

Mysterious Morning

Practice song answer for parents... Don't let your child see this answer at any time:

CHAPTER 6: Playing Chords in Music

LESSON 1

IDENTIFYING THE C CHORD IN MUSIC IN THE RIGHT HAND

C MAJOR CHORD

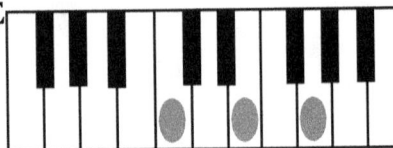

You have taught your child how to play a C chord on a piano. It looks like the image to the right. Now it is time to teach your child how to recognize a C chord in their music.

Any chord is a group of 3 notes. In music, those 3 notes are either all 3 line notes or all 3 space notes. A chord is made up of the first initial note and then a skip and then a skip again.

It is easy for a student to become overwhelmed at playing when they see three notes stacked on top of each other. Have them break it apart to make it simple to figure out.

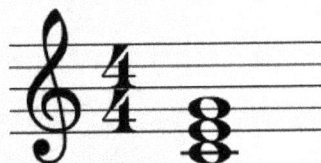

When your child sees three notes stacked on top of each other, for now, those notes will always be all skips. Have them figure out what the note on the very bottom is first. In the example to the right we see that the very bottom note is a middle C. The bottom notes tells us that it is a C major chord. Have your Child place their right hand on middle C and play a C major chord.

On this example to the right, we see that the bottom note of the chord is a C as well. However, this time the C is treble C. So in this example your child needs to place their hand on treble C and play a C chord there.

Show your child the examples above and have them play the examples on the piano in the correct location.

TEACHING THE PRACTICE SONG:

This song is in C position the whole song in both hands. Look over the music before beginning and point out where the notes step and where they skip.

This is a familiar tune, so it is extra important that all the counts are written in so it is played the way it is written and not the way your child might hear the music in their head. Make sure they observe all the rests and count aloud with a steady beat.

The three stacked notes in the right hand is the C major chord your child learned in this weeks lesson.

Daily Practice Log (4-6 days @ 15-20 minutes each day):
- ❋ *Flashcards for terms*
- ❋ *Flashcards for all notes (find the location on the piano)*
- ❋ *Practice song*
- ❋ *Corresponding Theory Chapter*
- ❋ *Hands together C & G Scale going up and down*
- ❋ *Flashcards all treble clef ledger lines combined*
- ❋ *Flashcard bass clef ledger line notes combined*
- ❋ *Play C, F, G // D, E, A // B major chord*
- ❋ *Play the D Scale hands together going up and down*

PRACTICE SONG lesson 1: Jingle Bells

Jingle Bells

ANSWERS FOR PARENTS

Jingle Bells

Practice song answer for parents... Don't let your child see this answer at any time:

LESSON 2

IDENTIFYING THE C CHORD IN MUSIC IN THE LEFT HAND

Recognizing the C chord in the left hand utilizes the same principles that you taught your child for the right hand. The only difference is your child needs to look for the bass clef symbol and use their left hand.

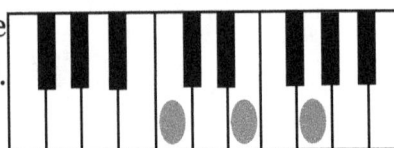

Any chord is a group of 3 notes. Those 3 notes are either all 3 line notes or all 3 space notes. A chord is made up of the first initial note and then a skip and then a skip again.

Have your child look at the example to the right. Explain to your child that we know the example to the right is a chord because it is a group of 3 notes stacked on top of each other with skips. Next, have them figure out what the bottom note they see is. They should answer it is the C from all **C**ows eat grass.

It is important that they recognize the C as bass C and play the C chord in that location.

TEACHING THE PRACTICE SONG:

Notice in this weeks practice song the 3 stacked notes periodically in the left hand. The bottom note of those stacks are all bass C. When you see that, make sure your child is playing a C chord.

The left hand crosses over the right hand in measure 3 and measure 11 to play the two A notes. After it plays those two A notes, it returns to the original LH C position.

Notice the pedal that starts in the beginning of the piece lets go at the end of measure 6. Remember when your child lets go of the pedal their heel should stay glued to the floor as the ball of their foot simply releases the pedal and rests on the pedal ready for the next time it plays.

Make sure that your child is playing contrary motion in measure 7 and also that they are holding the ties throughout the piece the correct number of beats.

152

Make sure to write in all the counts. There are a lot of rests make sure as your child counts to help them hold the tied notes for the correct amount of beats.

Daily Practice Log (4-6 days @ 15-20 minutes each day):
* *Flashcards for terms*
* *Flashcards for all notes (find the location on the piano)*
* *Practice song*
* *Corresponding Theory Chapter*
* *Hands together C & G Scale going up and down*
* *Flashcards all treble clef ledger lines combined*
* *Flashcard bass clef ledger line notes combined*
* *Play C, F, G //D, E, A // B major chord*
* *Play the D Scale hands together going up and down*

PRACTICE SONG lesson 2: Kumbaya

ANSWERS FOR PARENTS

Kumbaya

LESSON 3

IDENTIFYING THE G CHORD IN MUSIC IN THE RIGHT HAND

G MAJOR CHORD

Recognizing the G chord utilizes the same principles that you taught your child for the C chord. First have your child identify that it is three notes stacked on top of each other and those notes are either all line notes or all space notes.

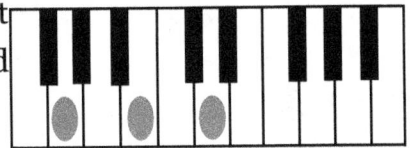

We see in the example to the right that the 3 notes are all line notes so we know its a chord. Now, have your child figure out what the bottom note of the chord is. They should answer G for every **G**ood boy deserves fudge. That means they are reading a G chord.

Have them play the G chord in the correct location on the piano.
They should be using their right hand because it is the treble clef and they should have their 1 finger on the G above middle C.

PLAYING WITH HALF RESTS

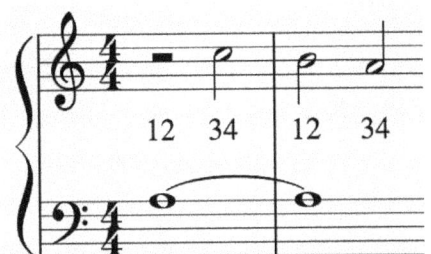

Your child has been doing their flashcard term for the half rest so they should be familiar that it gets 2 beats. When we see a half rest in the music we know that it gets 2 beats. Make sure your child counts 2 numbers. In the example to the right, the RH half rest gets beats 1-2 and then the note comes in on beat 3. Have your child play this example to the right for extra practice.

Daily Practice Log (4-6 days @ 15-20 minutes each day):

❋ *Flashcards for terms*
❋ *Flashcards for all notes (find the location on the piano)*
❋ *Practice song*
❋ *Corresponding Theory Chapter*
❋ *Hands together C & G Scale going up and down*
❋ *Flashcards all treble clef ledger lines combined*
❋ *Flashcard bass clef ledger line notes combined*
❋ *Play C, F, G //D, E, A // B major chord*
❋ *Play the D Scale hands together going up and down*

TEACHING THE PRACTICE SONG:

This weeks practice song starts out with the right hand playing the G chord that was in this weeks lesson. The left hand 5 finger is on the G below middle C. Notice the ledger line note D that is played by the 1 finger in the left hand. Ask your child where this note is located. They should answer that it is the D directly above middle C.

Make sure to write in all the counts. There are a lot of rests. Make sure as your child counts aloud that they observe the rests. This is especially tricky in measures like measure 4 where there is a half rest and the right hand doesn't come in until beat 3. Make sure your child counts two beats of Shh - Shh before coming in on beat 3.

PRACTICE SONG lesson 3: The Old Dirt Road

The Old Dirt Road

ANSWERS FOR PARENTS

The Old Dirt Road

Practice song answer for parents... Don't let your child see this answer at any time:

LESSON 4

IDENTIFYING THE G CHORD IN MUSIC IN THE LEFT HAND

In the example to the right, we see what we know to be a chord because it is three notes stacked on top of each other and they are all space notes. It might look scary to your child seeing this chord because there is a ledger line note in it. Don't have them focus on that part.

Have them do the same method as before. Ask them what is the bottom note of that chord they see? They should answer G for all cows eat **G**rass. That G is the G directly below middle C.

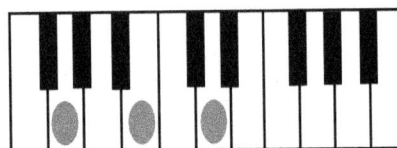

Have them play that chord using their left hand because they see the bass clef. Have them place the 5 finger on that G and play the G chord. If you notice, as your child plays the chord their thumb is on the D above middle C. That is the ledger line note you see in the chord in the example.

TEACHING THE PRACTICE SONG:

The right hand starts on the D above treble C with the 5 finger. Have your child identify where it skips and where it steps in the right hand.

The left hand has the 5 finger on the G below middle C and is playing the G chord that we learned in this lesson whenever they see three notes stacked on one another.

The rhythm in this song can be challenging so make sure to write in all the counts. Notice how throughout the song the right hand and left hand alternate playing. For example, in measure one on beat one there is a rest on the left hand while the right hand plays. Then on beat 2 there is a rest in the right hand while the left hand plays. There are a lot of rests make sure as your child counts that they observe the rests as they count aloud.

Daily Practice Log (4-6 days @ 15-20 minutes each day):

* ✺ *Flashcards for terms*
* ✺ *Flashcards for all notes (find the location on the piano)*
* ✺ *Practice song*
* ✺ *Corresponding Theory Chapter*
* ✺ *Hands together C & G Scale going up and down*
* ✺ *Flashcards all treble clef ledger lines combined*
* ✺ *Flashcard bass clef ledger line notes combined*
* ✺ *Play C, F, G //D, E, A // B major chord*
* ✺ *Play the D Scale hands together going up and down*

PRACTICE SONG lesson 4: Two Sisters

Two Sisters

ANSWERS FOR PARENTS

Three Sisters

Practice song answer for parents... Don't let your child see this answer at any time:

LESSON 5

IDENTIFYING THE F CHORD IN MUSIC IN THE RIGHT HAND

In the example to the right, we see what we know to be a chord because it is three notes stacked on top of each other and they are all space notes.

F MAJOR CHORD

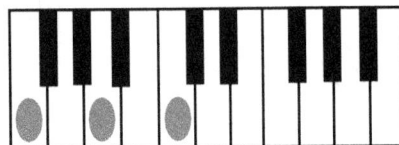

Have them do the same method as before. Ask them what is the bottom note of that chord they see? They should answer F for **FACE**. That F is the F directly above middle C.

Have them look at the example and play that chord using their right hand because they see the treble clef. Make sure they placed the 1 finger on that F note and played the F chord.

TEACHING THE PRACTICE SONG:

The right hand has the 1 finger on the F note above middle C. On this note your child plays the F chord that we learned in this lesson. Notice the tie that happen in measure 1. Notice that each note of the chord (the F, the A, the C) all have a tie leading from it to the next chord. This means to tie/hold every note of the F chord for 2 full measures.

The left hand has the 5 finger on the F below middle C. Remember each white note gets one finger assigned to it. So when your left hand has a B-flat in the music that will be played with the 2 finger.

Be careful your child observes the ties in the left hand as well as the tie over the measure's bar line. Make sure to write in all the counts and then have your child count aloud to help them observe all the tied notes.

Daily Practice Log (4-6 days @ 15-20 minutes each day):

- ✸ *Flashcards for terms*
- ✸ *Flashcards for all notes (find the location on the piano)*
- ✸ *Practice song*
- ✸ *Corresponding Theory Chapter*
- ✸ *Hands together C & G Scale going up and down*
- ✸ *Flashcards all treble clef ledger lines combined*
- ✸ *Flashcard bass clef ledger line notes combined*
- ✸ *Play C, F, G //D, E, A // B major chord*
- ✸ *Play the D Scale hands together going up and down*

PRACTICE SONG lesson 5: Salt and Pepper

Salt and Pepper

Stephanie Parker

ANSWERS FOR PARENTS

Salt and Pepper

Practice song answer for parents... Don't let your child see this answer at any time:

LESSON 6

IDENTIFYING THE F CHORD IN MUSIC IN THE LEFT HAND

In the example to the right, we see what we know to be a chord because it is three notes stacked on top of each other and they are all line notes. It might look scary to your child seeing this chord because there is what looks to be a ledger line at the top. It is actually just the note middle C at the top.

F MAJOR CHORD

Regardless, have them do the same method as before. Ask them what is the bottom note of that chord they see? They should answer F for grizzly bears don't **F**ly airplanes. That F is the F directly below middle C.

Have them look at the example to the right and play that chord using their left hand because they see the bass clef. Make sure they placed the 5 finger on that F note and played the F chord.

TEACHING THE PRACTICE SONG:

This song plays all the chords your child has learned to recognize in this chapter. It starts with a G chord then goes to a F chord and ends finally on the C chord.

Notice that first the chord is played broken. A broken chord simply means that the notes of the chord are played one at a time. So we hear first G then B then D in the right hand then left hand. Then we see those same notes stacked so we know then to play those same notes but now all at the same time (a chord) instead of separate (broken chord).

The left hand has a ledger line D above middle C played during the broken and regular chord of the G chord section.

In each new broken chord section, both hands have a hand shift even though it isn't written into the music. Make sure the hands shift so that they are in the proper hand position of playing the chords and chord broken notes with only the 1-3-5 fingers.

This song is in 3/4 time. Make sure to write in all the counts. There are a lot of rests. Make sure as your child counts aloud that they observe the rests.

Daily Practice Log (4-6 days @ 15-20 minutes each day):
* ❋ *Flashcards for all notes (find the location on the piano)*
* ❋ *Practice song*
* ❋ *Corresponding Theory Chapter*
* ❋ *Hands together C & G Scale going up and down*
* ❋ *Flashcards all treble clef ledger lines combined*
* ❋ *Flashcard bass clef ledger line notes combined*
* ❋ *C,F,G // D,E,A // B major chords.*
* ❋ *Play the D scale RH going up & down*
* ❋ *Play the D scale LH going up*
* ❋ *Play D scale going up & down hands together*

PRACTICE SONG lesson 6: The Chorded Lullaby

The Chorded Lullaby

ANSWERS FOR PARENTS

The Chorded Lullaby

Practice song answer for parents... Don't let your child see this answer at any time:

How To Teach Your Child Piano - Level 2

CHAPTER 7: Practicing Major Chords

LESSON 1

F MAJOR SCALE IN THE RIGHT HAND GOING UP

Your child has learned the C,G and D scale and can play them hands together going up and down. The next scale we will learn is the F scale.

The F scale has 1 black note: the B♭. So, instead of playing a white note on B you will need to play the black note BELOW this note to the LEFT.

The C scale had 0 black notes, the G scale had 1 black note - F#, the D scale has 2 black notes - F# and C#, and the F scale has one black note - B♭. Make sure your child can verbally articulate this. Ask them before they play each of their scales in their lesson/ practice time these two questions:

      1) How many black notes are in this scale?
      2) What are they?

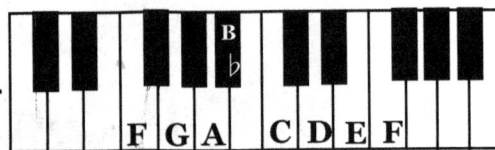

The image to the right shows what the F major

F MAJOR SCALE

scale looks like on the piano and which notes are played in the F scale.

The F scale uses the exact same fingering all the other scales your child has learned so far in the left hand, but it is very different fingering in the right hand.

In the right hand, instead of having the 1 finger tunnel under after the 3 finger, This scale changes that. In the RIGHT HAND ONLY the tunnel happens after the 4 finger. It can be a bit of a stretch for a student to have their 4 finger on the B♭ and then tunnel under all the way to the C note. They often try to play the white note B note instead with their 1 finger.

Be careful that they don't tunnel the 1 finger to the B white note, but instead make their thumb reach all the way under to the C note. When tunneling under on this scale students often contort their arm in weird positions to reach the C. Be careful that your student maintains proper arm posture as they tunnel under with their shoulders relaxed, elbows at their sides and wrist not too high or too low.

Once they reach the C with their 1 finger have them shift their hand so that their fingers are all in line with the new position of the 1 finger. The rest of the notes are fairly easy to play. The part to pay attention to is that **the pinky is not used in this RH scale**. The 1 finger plays C, the 2 plays D, the 3 plays E and the 4 plays F. That's it. You've reached the top of this scale.

Make sure they don't keep playing to use up all their fingers like they are used to and continue on to the G note with their pinky. The pinky does not get used in the right hand of this scale.

This week, have your child play the right hand F scale going up only. Below are the notes and fingering for this scale in the Right hand going up. The large number is where the thumb tunnels under after the 4.

F-G-A-B♭-C-D-E-F

The right hand finger numbers going up for this scale is: 1- 2-3 -4 - 1-2-3-4

Notice that the 4 plays the B♭ and the tunnel happens AFTER the B♭.

A NEW WAY TO PRACTICE MAJOR CHORDS: C-D

Up until now when your child has practiced their major chords they have separated them and played the 3 all white note ones (C,F,G), then the 3 with the black note in the middle (D,E,A), then the last tricky one with 2 black notes (B).

Continue to have them practice this method until we finish this chapter. By the end of the chapter your child will be able to play them Going up the keyboard in this order:
C major - D major - E major - F major - G major - A major - B major.

This week we will start with being able to play just the first two. Get your child used to playing from C major to D major. Make sure they are counting the 3 skipped half steps in each chord to know that it goes

C MAJOR CHORD   D MAJOR CHORD

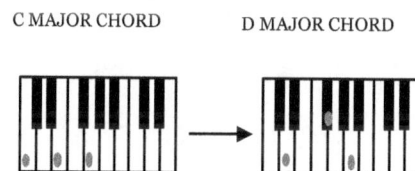

from an all white chord to a chord with a black note in the middle as demonstrated in the image to the right.

TEACHING THE PRACTICE SONG:

This song starts with your child's right hand in a different position than they have been in so far. The music says to put the 2 finger on F#. That would mean that the 1 finger is on the note E above middle C.

Remember each white note is assigned one finger. So 1 is on E, 2 is on F#, that means 3 is on G.

G is the second note of the song in the right hand and should be played with the 3 finger.

The left hand crosses over the right hand in measures 4,8,17 and 21. When it crosses over it plays a single note with the left hand 2 finger and then it goes back to its normal position on the piano.

Before beginning to play the song, point out to your child that the left hand moves positions throughout the song. The very first measure the bottom note of the chord is a G so it is a G chord.

In measure 5 it moves to a new chord and in measure 9 it moves again this time putting a 4 finger on the D note. At the beginning of each line, the left hand moves positions. There is no "hand shift" written into the music until the very last note, so make sure your child is carefully reading each of those notes.

There is pedal that starts and ends on each line except for line 3 where there is no pedal. Make sure your child releases the pedal at the end of each line, but does not remove their heel from the floor when doing so. Do not have them learn to play the song with the pedal until they have mastered everything else. Pedal is a last step.

Make sure to write in all the counts. Have your child count aloud and observe the rests.

Daily Practice Log (4-6 days @ 15-20 minutes each day):
- *Flashcards for terms*
- *Flashcards for all notes (find the location on the piano)*
- *Practice song*
- *Corresponding Theory Chapter*
- *Hands together C & G Scale going up and down*
- *Flashcards all treble clef ledger lines combined*
- *Flashcard bass clef ledger line notes combined*
- *Play C, F, G //D, E, A // B major chord*
- *Play the D Scale hands together going up and down*
- *Play the F Scale RH going up.*
- *Play Major chords C to D*

PRACTICE SONG lesson 1: Morning Dew

Morning Dew

Stephanie Parker

Morning Dew

Practice song answer for parents... Don't let your child see this answer at any time:

179

LESSON 2

F MAJOR SCALE IN THE RIGHT HAND GOING UP AND DOWN

To learn the scale heading in the downward direction first have your child go up the scale and hold the F at the top. Then have them go back down. Remember that they should be on a 4 finger at the top of the scale and the 5 is not used. **F MAJOR SCALE RH**

The finger pattern for going down the scale is different than we have done for every other scale.

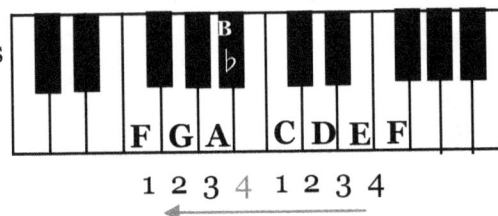

All the other scales have had the 3rd finger bunny hop over. In the F scale RIGHT HAND ONLY it is the FOUR finger that bunny hops over the 1 finger.

Make sure when it bunny hops over it bunny hops all the way to the B ♭ note.

Below are the notes and fingering for this scale in the Right hand going down. The large number is where the 4 bunny hops over the 1.

F-E-D-C-B ♭ -A-G-F

4 32 1 4   3 2 1

Once that makes sense to your child have your child practice independently going up and down the F scale.

GOING UP   F-G-A-B ♭ -C-D-E-F

1 2 3 4 1 2 3 4

GOING DOWN   F-E-D-C-B ♭ -A-G-F

4 32 1 4   3 2 1

NEW WAY TO PRACTICE MAJOR CHORDS: C-E

This week your child will learn to play the first 3 chords of their major chords in the bolded order below:

C major - D major - E major - (not yet: F major - G major - A major - B major).

Your child should be used to playing from C major to D major. Once they get to the D chord have them continue the the E major chord next. Make sure they are counting the 3 skipped half steps in each chord to know that it goes from an all white chord to a chord with a black note in the middle to another chord with a black note in the middle. The order of this weeks chord practice is demonstrated in the image below.

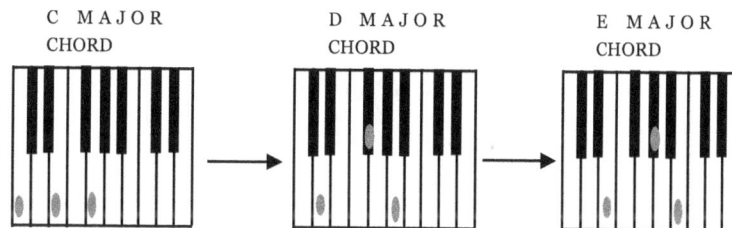

During practice time have them do the old separated method for review and then have them play C through E major chords as listed above.

TEACHING THE PRACTICE SONG:

The first note we see in the right hand is the F note from the saying FACE. There is a 3 finger above it telling the student to place their 3rd finger on the F note. There is a hand shift for the right hand in measure 7 & 10 where you child needs to be extra cautious that the correct finger is playing the correct note in the correct location.

The left hand begins with the 1 finger on middle C and never moves from this location. Be careful in the left hand of the long extended ties and also that the 2 finger is the one playing all B-flat notes.

This is a familiar tune. Make sure your child is playing it the way it is written and not the way they think it should sound. To accomplish this goal have them write in all the counts and count aloud as they play.

Daily Practice Log (4-6 days @ 15-20 minutes each day):
- ❋ *Flashcards for terms*
- ❋ *Flashcards for all notes (find the location on the piano)*
- ❋ *Practice song*
- ❋ *Corresponding Theory Chapter*
- ❋ *Hands together C & G & D Scale going up and down*
- ❋ *Flashcards all treble clef ledger lines combined*
- ❋ *Flashcard bass clef ledger line notes combined*
- ❋ *Play C, F, G //D, E, A // B major chord*
- ❋ *Play the F Scale RH going up and down*
- ❋ *Major chords order C to E*

PRACTICE SONG lesson 2: Amazing Grace

Amazing Grace

ANSWERS FOR PARENTS

Practice song answer for parents... Don't let your child see this answer at any time:

LESSON 3

F MAJOR SCALE IN THE LEFT HAND GOING UP

Unlike the right hand, the left hand F scale follows the same pattern as all the other LH scales we have

F MAJOR SCALE LH

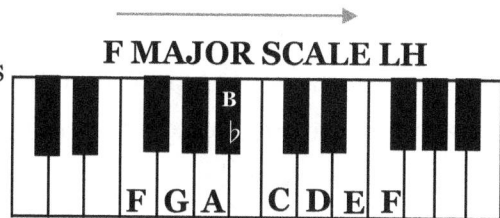

5 4 3 2 1 3 2 1

learned. That means your fingering going up will be 5-4-3-2-1-3-2-1. The thing to watch out for is that your child goes from A to B♭ to C in the middle of the scale.

Below are the notes and fingering for this scale in the left hand going up. The large number is where the 3 bunny hops over the 1.

F-G-A-B♭-C-D-E-F

5 4 3 2 1 3 2 1

NEW WAY TO PRACTICE MAJOR CHORDS: C-F

This week your child will learn to play the first 4 chords of their major chords in the bolded order below:

C major - D major - E major - F major - (not yet: G major - A major - B major).

Your child should be used to playing from C to E major. Once they get to the E chord have them continue to the F major chord next. Make sure they are counting the 3 skipped half steps in each chord to know which type of chord they should be playing. The correct progression is in the image below.

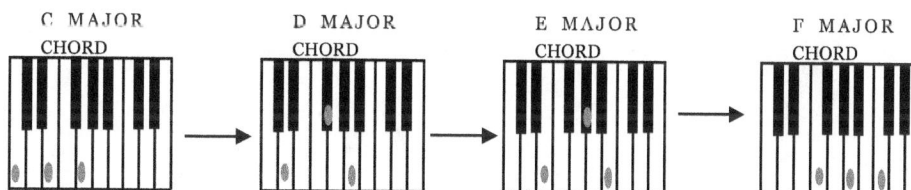

During practice time, have them do the old separated method for review and then have them play C through F major chords as listed above.

TEACHING THE PRACTICE SONG:

This weeks song has the right hand in C position for the first line. The first group of notes that are played are the top two notes of the C chord (E & G). That is followed by the bottom two notes of the C chord (C & E). Notice that the E is played in both of groups of notes.

This same pattern is repeated on the second line, but in a new location and with a new chord. The Right hand should move its 5 finger to the D above middle C. It is a line to line skip. The group of notes that should be played together here are the top two notes of the G chord (B & D). Then it is followed by the bottom two notes of the G chord (G & B). Notice that the middle note of the chord, B, is played in both groups of notes.

Then, in the last line it returns to a C chord to play the original pattern that we saw in line 1.

The left hand starts in C position, just like the right hand. Also like the right hand, each time the right hand shifts positions so does the left hand.

The left hand does steps and skips. Look over the music before playing and make sure your child recognizes where it steps and where it skips.

Have them learn this song hands apart before attempting to learn it hands together. This song is in 3/4. Make sure to write in all the counts and count aloud.

Daily Practice Log (4-6 days @ 15-20 minutes each day):

* ✺ *Flashcards for terms*
* ✺ *Flashcards for all notes (find the location on the piano)*
* ✺ *Practice song*
* ✺ *Corresponding Theory Chapter*
* ✺ *Hands together C & G & D Scale going up and down*
* ✺ *Flashcards all treble clef ledger lines combined*
* ✺ *Flashcard bass clef ledger line notes combined*
* ✺ *Play C, F, G //D, E, A // B major chord*
* ✺ *Play the F Scale RH going up and down*
* ✺ *Play the F scale LH going up*
* ✺ *Major chords order C to F*

PRACTICE SONG lesson 3: A Simple Waltz

A Simple Waltz

ANSWERS FOR PARENTS

A Simple Waltz

Practice song answer for parents... Don't let your child see this answer at any time:

LESSON 4

F MAJOR SCALE IN THE LEFT HAND GOING UP AND DOWN

To learn the scale heading in the downward direction in the left hand first have your child go up the scale and hold the F at the top, then have them go back down.

F MAJOR SCALE LH

The finger pattering for the LH going down the scale is the exact same finger patter for the LH C scale heading down. Just be careful that after your child plays the C, they play the B♭ next.

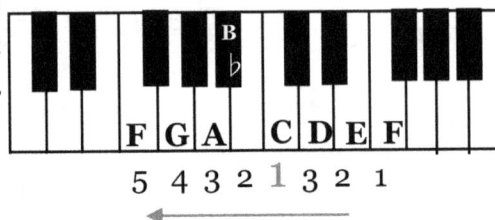

Below are the notes and fingering for this scale in the left hand going down. The large number is where the 1 finger tunnels under the 3 finger.

F-E-D-C-B♭-A-G-F

1 2 3 1 2 3 4 5

Once that makes sense to your child have your child practice independently going up and down the G scale in the left hand.

GOING UP   F-G-A-B♭-C-D-E-F

                                   5 4 3 2 1 3 2 1

GOING DOWN   F-E-D-C-B♭-A-G-F

                                   1 2 3 1 2 3 4 5

NEW WAY TO PRACTICE MAJOR CHORDS: C-G

This week your child will learn to play the first 5 chords of their major chords in the bolded order below:

C major - D major - E major - F major - G major - (not yet: A major - B major).

Your child should be used to playing from C to F major. Once they get to the F chord have them continue to the G major chord next. Make sure they are counting the 3 skipped half steps in each chord to know which type of chord they should be playing. The correct progression is in the image below.

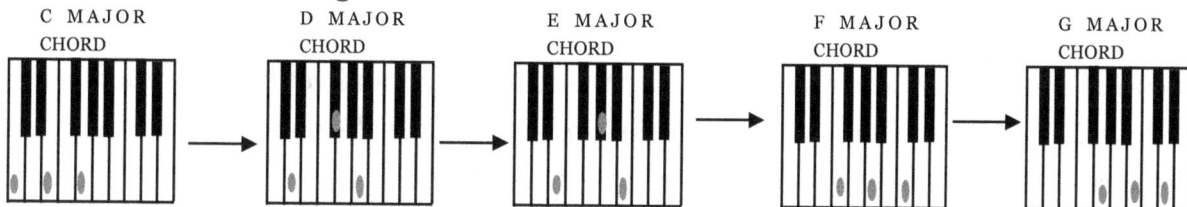

During practice time have them do the old separated method for review and then have them play C through G major chords.

TEACHING THE PRACTICE SONG:

This song is unique in that the right hand doesn't begin until line 2. On line 2 the right hand needs to have its 5 finger on the B and the 3rd finger on the skip below that: G. In measure 6, notice that the two line notes BOTH step down to two space notes. That means the notes right next G & B will play.

Remind your child that when a step occurs you use the very next finger numbers. So If a 3 & 5 are playing then the step will have the 2 & 4 playing. The 2 will be on the F# and the 4 will be on the A. This fingering occurs everywhere there is a F# in the right hand in the song.

There is a hand shift in the right hand in measure 5. At this point in the music, the right hand 5 finger needs to play the E above middle C. On the last line the RH shifts back to the original position for the remainder of the song.

Take time to learn just the right hand.

The left hand has a very tricky note and rhythm pattern. However, once your child masters the first couple of measures they have learned the entire left hand as it repeats the same thing over and over the whole song.

Spend a lot of time mastering the left hand hands apart. Mastering the left hand before adding the right hand to it will make it so much easier for your child to put hands together.

The way the rests work within the song is more complex than we have done. You child can do it, just follow the steps of the best way to learn complex music and they will be fine.

Write in all the counts. Make sure they clap the RH rhythm and get it really good before moving on. Then, have them clap the LH rhythm and get it really good before moving on. Make sure they can count it aloud as they clap it hands apart as well as when they move on to playing it hands apart. Have them continue to count it aloud as they slowly begin to put the song hands together.

Daily Practice Log (4-6 days @ 15-20 minutes each day):
- *Flashcards for terms*
- *Flashcards for all notes (find the location on the piano)*
- *Practice song*
- *Corresponding Theory Chapter*
- *Hands together C & G & D Scale going up and down*
- *Flashcards all treble clef ledger lines combined*
- *Flashcard bass clef ledger line notes combined*
- *Play C, F, G // D, E, A // B major chord*
- *Play the F Scale RH going up and down*
- *Play the F Scale LH going up and down*
- *Play the F scale Hands together going up*
- *Major chords order C to A*

Stephanie Parker

PRACTICE SONG lesson 4: Duel of el Gato

Duel of el Gato

Duel of el Gato

LESSON 5

F MAJOR SCALE HANDS TOGETHER GOING UP

You have taught your child to play the F scale hands apart. If they still struggle hands apart, really focus on the scale practice so they can master it and move on to this step of playing the F scale in both hands at the same time.

Before beginning, remind your child that the LH will be the same fingering as all the other scales, but the RH has a new fingering that tunnels after the 4 finger on the way up.
Here is what that will look like:

$$F - G - A - B♭ - C - D - E - F$$

RIGHT HAND:	1 2 3 4 1 2 3 4
LEFT HAND:	5 4 3 2 1 3 2 1

Notice that the "tunnel" and the "bunny hop" do not happen at the exact same time. First comes the tunnel followed later by the bunny hop.

When teaching this to your child take it slow. Have them play just the F's together. Once they do that with ease, then have them play F's to G's together. Once that happens have them do the first 3 notes together (F-G-A).

This is where it'll get harder. While both hands are on the A note have them go in both hands the the B♭ playing it with the 4 finger in the right hand and the 2 finger in the left hand.

Now, have them just hold the note down B♭ and really talk through what will happen next. Next the left hand will play the 1 finger on the C, but the right hand will have the thumb tunnel under to the C (make sure they tunnel all the way to C and don't hit the B white note).
When they master playing the C's together, pause. Make sure they shifted their whole right hand in line with the new thumb position. If everything looks right move on to the D's.

Here comes the bunny hop. To play the D the LH is out of fingers, so it will need to bunny hop over the C which is being held with the 1 finger in order to play the D with finger 3. Have the D's play simultaneously with both hands. Then, shift the left hand to be in line with the new position of the third finger.

For the rest, your child's hand is in position and ready to play the D's together and then the E's together then the F's together.

Your right hand should have landed on the the F note with the 4th finger leaving the pinky (5 finger) unused in this scale in the right hand.

Stop here. Don't try and go down the scale yet. Do this scale going up a couple more times throughout the lesson until you're sure you child will be able to practice it during the week.

At this stage, do not have your child go straight to hands together practice each day with the F scale. Have them play the right hand scale up and down, then the left hand scale up and down. Then have them do hands together going up only.

NEW WAY TO PRACTICE MAJOR CHORDS: C-A

This week your child will learn to play the first 6 chords of their major chords in the bolded order below:
C major - D major - E major - F major - G major - A major - (not yet: B major).

Your child should be used to playing from C to G major. Once they get to the G chord have them continue to the A major chord next. Make sure they are counting the 3 skipped half steps in each chord to know which type of chord they should be playing. The correct progression is in the image below.

During practice time have them do the old separated method for review and then have them play C through A major chords.

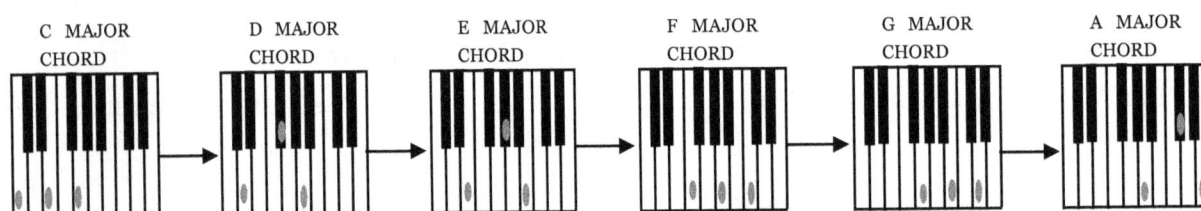

C MAJOR CHORD → D MAJOR CHORD → E MAJOR CHORD → F MAJOR CHORD → G MAJOR CHORD → A MAJOR CHORD

TEACHING THE PRACTICE SONG:

The right hand position is the same as last weeks song. The 3 & 5 finger need to be on the G & B notes. The 2 & 4 notes will play when it steps down to F# & A.

The left hand is a 4th finger on the D note above bass C. Neither hand moves from its original position in the song.

What to look out for in this song is the way the left hand and right hand alternate playing due to the rests. To make sure this is done correctly have your child write in all the counts and count aloud first hands apart then hands together.

Daily Practice Log (4-6 days @ 15-20 minutes each day):
- ❀ *Flashcards for terms*
- ❀ *Flashcards for all notes (find the location on the piano)*
- ❀ *Practice song*
- ❀ *Corresponding Theory Chapter*
- ❀ *Hands together C & G & D Scale going up and down*
- ❀ *Flashcards all treble clef ledger lines combined*
- ❀ *Flashcard bass clef ledger line notes combined*
- ❀ *Play C, F, G //D, E, A // B major chord*
- ❀ *Play the F Scale RH going up and down*
- ❀ *Play the F Scale LH going up and down*
- ❀ *Play the F scale hands together going up and down*
- ❀ *Major chords order C to B*

Liz's Lazy Horse

Stephanie Parker

ANSWERS FOR PARENTS

Liz's Lazy Horse

Practice song answer for parents... Don't let your child see this answer at any time:

LESSON 6

F MAJOR SCALE HANDS TOGETHER GOING UP AND DOWN

If your child is able to go up the F scale hands together, then move on to teaching them this week about coming back down the scale. If going up the scale hands together is still a challenge for them, give them another week or two just going up hands together and then at that time return to this part of lesson 6.

Just like when they went up the scale the two hands did the opposite of one another (one tunneled and the other one bunny hopped), the same thing will happen going down except the two hands will switch which one they're doing.

On the way down, the right hand will bunny hop when it runs out of fingers and the left hand will tunnel under after the 3 finger.

The best way to teach going down the scale is to have them go up the scale hands together and stop when they get to the top on that F and rest there (RH should be resting on the 4th finger). Now you will talk them through each note.

For the first three notes, your child's fingers are exactly where they should be. So have them go down playing the F's together then the E's together then the D's together and then have them pause holding down the D's.

On the D, the left hand is on the 3 finger, so it will need to have the 1 finger (thumb) tunnel under to the C. Once its in position, have BOTH hands play the C's at the same time and then shift the left hand to be in position with the new thumb location.

Once the C's have played, the right hand has run out of fingers. This means the right hand now needs to have the 4th finger bunny hop over the thumb and get into position to play the B♭. Once it's in position have the two hands play the B♭'s at the same time. Then have the right hand shift the hand so its in position with the new location of the 4th finger.

The last three notes are all lined up and ready to go, so have them play the A's then the G's together and then the F's together.

If your child catches on to this concept fairly quickly, they can go straight to hands together F scale in their practice time. If it is a bit of a struggle still, then have their scale practice time be:

1) RH hands apart F scale up and down
2) LH hands apart F scale up and down
3) Hands together F scale up and down.

NEW WAY TO PRACTICE MAJOR CHORDS: C-B

This week your child will learn to play all of their major chords in order:
C major - D major - E major - F major - G major - A major - B major.

Your child should be used to playing from C to A major. Once they get to the A chord have them continue to the B major chord next. Make sure they are counting the 3 skipped half steps in each chord to know which type of chord they should be playing. The correct progression is in the image below.

If they are able to do this correctly change their chord practice to going in this order right away every time. There is no more need to separate their chords during practice. If this concept is still a challenge for them, then have the first do the separated method of chord practice followed by the C thru B chord progression until they are confident enough going C through B to eliminate the separated method of practice.

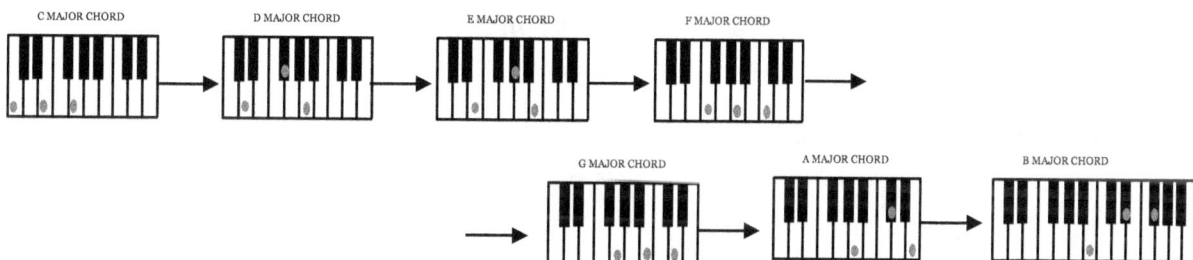

TEACHING THE PRACTICE SONG:

This weeks practice song has the left hand playing intervals of a 3rd in each measure. The starting note of the intervals of a 3rd change in each measure. The pattern that is in the left hand on the first line repeats for the entire song. Have your child really master this pattern hands apart and it will make putting it hands together much easier for them.

The right hand comes in on line 2 in the normal RH C position and it stays there the entire song. Line 2 and line 5 has intervals of a 3rd in the RH; however, the intervals in the right hand are skipping down in each measure.

Make sure to have your child write in all the counts and count aloud.

Daily Practice Log (4-6 days @ 15-20 minutes each day):
- *Flashcards for terms*
- *Flashcards for all notes (find the location on the piano)*
- *Practice song*
- *Corresponding Theory Chapter*
- *Hands together C & G & D & F Scale going up and down*
- *Flashcards all treble clef ledger lines combined*
- *Flashcard bass clef ledger line notes combined*
- *Major chords order C to B*

PRACTICE SONG lesson 6: A Walk in the Rain

A Walk in the Rain

A Walk in the Rain

CHAPTER 8: Putting it all Together

LESSON 1

BOTH HANDS PLAYING TREBLE CLEF

By this point, your child is used to reading a grand staff. It is the image to the right. We know that the top line has a treble clef is played by the right hand and the bottom line has a bass clef is played by the left hand.

a n d
a n d

The rules of the grand staff applies to all music you see. The top line is always the line that is played by the right hand and the bottom line of the grand staff is always the line that is played by the left hand.

With that rule in mind, sometimes our music doesn't always have the bottom line have a bass clef symbol. Sometimes music can have both lines have treble clef symbols like the image to the right. What does that mean? Does that mean both hands should be played by the right hand? No, that's impossible.

If both lines of the grand staff have the treble clef symbol, it still follows the rule: the top line is played by the right hand and the bottom hand is played by the left hand. What is different is the left hand's location on the piano. The clef symbol is really just a location marker. It tells you **where** the note should be played on the piano.

When the left hand staff has a treble clef, we would read the notes like it is a treble clef flashcard. For example, look at the image below. The Right hand (Top staff) note is fairly simply to read. It is a treble C, so your child would place their finger on the C above middle C.

The left hand note is harder at first to read. Cover up the top RH staff and ask your child to read the bottom staff. Tell them to pretend this is all they saw. Tell them to pretend this was a flashcard. In that case, what would the note be? Thinking of it like that makes it easier for them to see that the note is middle C.

Remove your hand and show them it is still a middle C even though it is written as the bottom section of the grand staff. Have them play the notes in the example to the right in the correct location with each hand.

Let's do another example before this weeks practice song. In the example to the right, have your child figure out the note on the top, RH. Did they say it is the note E from FACE? Now have them figure out the correct location on the piano. If they struggle with this as them questions to help them get to the answer. For example, ask them, "where is treble C on the staff? Is this note above or below treble C?" They should see that the note is above treble C; therefore, it is the E above treble C.

The left hand note is the bottom line of the staff. Have them figure out the note this time without covering up the top line if possible. Did they say it was an E from every good boy deserves fudge? Ask them where the location of this E is on the piano. If they struggle to realize where its location is, ask them where middle C would be drawn on the staff. You can also pull out your middle C flashcard if they struggle to grasp the question. Once they realize where middle C is, it is easier to tell that the E in the image is the E above middle C. Have them play the notes in the example to the above in the correct location with each hand.

TEACHING THE PRACTICE SONG:

The right hand is playing a 2 finger on treble C. It never moves from this position.

The left hand is reading the treble clef. It is a chord, so have your child identify the bottom note of the chord. Remember to have them pretend they are reading RH flashcards. Cover over the top line if that helps them figure out the Bottom note of the chord.

Once they identify the bottom note as middle C, point out to them that it is 3 notes stacked together on all lines. Ask them what that means? They should answer that it means they are playing a chord. The left hand is playing a C chord build on middle C the whole song.

Make sure to have them write in all the counts and count aloud as they play.

Daily Practice Log (4-6 days @ 15-20 minutes each day):

 ✻ *Flashcards for terms*
 ✻ *Flashcards for all notes (find the location on the piano)*
 ✻ *Practice song*
 ✻ *Corresponding Theory Chapter*
 ✻ *Hands together C & G & D & F Scale going up and down*
 ✻ *Flashcards all treble clef ledger lines combined*
 ✻ *Flashcard bass clef ledger line notes combined*
 ✻ *Major chords order C to B*

Stephanie Parker

PRACTICE SONG lesson 1: My Country

My Country

My Country

Practice song answer for parents... Don't let your child see this answer at any time

LESSON 2

BOTH HANDS PLAYING TREBLE CLEF

In the last lesson you taught your child how to read the music when both hands play the treble clef. However the music had the left hand stay somewhat stationary through the song. What happens when the left hand has more movement during a song with two treble clefs? The same principle applies in that your left hand plays the bottom notes, but reads the notes as if they are the treble clef flashcards.

This can be hard to do quickly for a beginner student when there are moving notes. For that reason, show your child even if the notes are hard to comprehend quickly, the can follow the musical pattern rules they have already learned: notes going up go up the piano, notes going down go down the piano, a space to a line is a step, and a line to a line or a space to a space is a skip.

Have them play the example to the right. Remember, difficult songs should be learned hands apart before playing both hands at the same time. Have them learn to play just the right hand. Then, have then learn to play just the left hand. Then put both the hands together to play them at the same time. Below is the answer of what they should have played (don't let them see the answer, just use it for your reference to check their understanding of the concept.

PLAYING A RIT.

Your child has already been studying in their flashcard terms the term Rit. Which means ritardando - to slow down gradually.

In the example to the right, we see it applied to their music for the first time. The way it would work is the first measure is played completely normally. The 1st beat of the 2nd measure is also played normally. The beat/note where the Rit. Is placed is where the slow down begins. In this example, on the last three notes, each one plays together and each one goes slower than the one before it getting slower and slower.

TEACHING THE PRACTICE SONG:

Just like last weeks song, this song has the right hand with the 2 finger on the treble C, the C above middle C. Notice the half rest in measure 7. It starts on beat 2. Remember a half rest gets 2 beats or 2 numbers. Since the half rest starts on beat 2 that means it will count beats 2-3 during the rest.

The left hand is the bottom line of the grand staff even though it's the treble clef symbol. Have your child figure out what that note name would be. If they are struggling, cover with your hand the top line and tell them pretend it's the right hand. What would the note be?

Once they figure out what the note is ask them where on the piano the note would be located. It is the E above middle C. Have them place their 4 finger on the E above middle C for the left hand line.

Notice the rests in measure 7. The rests occur on beat 1 and beat 4. That means the two quarter notes take place on beat 2 and 3. In measure 7, the RH plays while the LH rests and the LH plays while the RH rests. Make sure they write in the counts for the whole song and count aloud paying close attention to these rests.

212

There is a lot of movement in both hands for this song. Have them learn it hands apart and get it very good before they attempt to put it hands together. Talk through the song with your child regarding steps and skips. Point out in measures 1-5 where the right hand and left hand mirror each other even though they are on different notes. Both hands either step together or skip together. It isn't until measure 6 that there is some contrary motion between the two hands.

Daily Practice Log (4-6 days @ 15-20 minutes each day):
* *Flashcards for terms*
* *Flashcards for all notes (find the location on the piano)*
* *Practice song*
* *Corresponding Theory Chapter*
* *Hands together C & G & D & F Scale going up and down*
* *Flashcards all treble clef ledger lines combined*
* *Flashcard bass clef ledger line notes combined*
* *Major chords order C to B*

PRACTICE SONG lesson 2: Yankee Doodle

Yankee Doodle

ANSWERS FOR PARENTS

Yankee Doodle

Practice song answer for parents... Don't let your child see this answer at any time

LESSON 3

PLAYING THE G's ON THE PIANO

Your child learned about bass, middle and treble C. The same concept can be applied to other notes as well. In the image to the right, we see a treble G above a middle C. There's a middle G which is right below middle C. Then, theres a bass G which is the G below middle G.

We can also know the location of bass G because you can have your child identify where bass C would be located and determine if the note they see in their music is above or below that location.

PLAYING A BASS G CHORD

The chord to the right is a G chord. We know that because, like all chords, we look at the bottom note and whatever the name of that note is, that's the name of our chord. The bottom of the chord to the right is a G from grizzly bears don't fly airplanes.

Once your child figured out the type of chord, have them determine the location. It is not the middle G close to middle C on the top of the staff. It is the bass G below that. So when they see a G chord that looks like the image to the right make sure they build it off the Bass G location.

TEACHING THE PRACTICE SONG:

This weeks song has a lot of movement in the left hand from middle G note to the bass G chord. Have your child identify all the middle G's in the song and then all the bass G's in the song. Also point out in the LH how it isn't only the G chord that is played, but there is also a C chord also played.

Watch the rhythm in measure 4 where the half note in the left hand precedes the note. Remember the half note gets 2 beats so the note should not be played until the beat of 3. That rhythm in the LH happens several times throughout the song.

There are also ties throughout the song that hold over the barline, so make sure your child writes in their counts. Have them learn to count it aloud RH alone, then count it aloud LH alone before putting it hands together counting it aloud.

Daily Practice Log (4-6 days @ 15-20 minutes each day):
* *Flashcards for all notes (find the location on the piano for some of them)*
* *Practice song*
* *Corresponding Theory Chapter*
* *Hands together C Then G Scale going up and down*
* *Flashcard all treble clef ledger line notes combined*
* *Flashcard all bass clef ledger line notes combined*
* *C,F,G // D,E,A // B major chords.*
* *Play the D scale RH going up & down*
* *Play the D scale LH going up*

PRACTICE SONG lesson 3: Aloutte

Aloutte

ANSWERS FOR PARENTS

Aloutte

Practice song answer for parents... Don't let your child see this answer at any time:

LESSON 4

MEMORIZING A SONG

The best way to memorize is 1 measure at a time. Have them look at the music for measure 1, then play it without their music. Once they can play measure 1 without their music, have them look at their music for measure 2. Then have them play just measure 2 without their music. Then have them look at their music and play measures 1-2. Then have them play by memory measures 1-2. Once they accomplish that, add measure 3. Once measure 3 is memorized by itself add then learn to play measures 1-3 by memory. Continue with this memory method until the whole song is learned.

Once their song is memorized and can be played close to perfectly, have a recital. This can be done via zoom with family and friends or it can be done in your home having family and friends over or it can have both done simultaneously.

PREPARING FOR A RECITAL

This book should take 6-12 months to complete... basically one school year. At the end of each school year teachers typically have a piano recital. One of the best motivational tools for a child to not only continue with piano lessons, but also enjoy and look forward to lessons is the yearly recital.

At a recital, they can tangibly see the fruits of their labor. They see that they worked really hard and then they were able to create something really beautiful and they were celebrated for their hard work by their friends and family that come to the recital.

Just because you are teaching your child piano at home does not mean your child has to miss out on this experience! When your child finishes the last lesson of this book, have them really master the practice song. Spend a longer than average amount of time on the last song making sure it is pretty much without mistake.

Take several weeks to master this weeks lesson song. Get the song to the point where it is almost easy for your child to play well. Even if it takes 3-4 weeks or longer that is ok. It is normal to take longer on a song that will be performed for a recital. Use the time mastering this song to solidify all the skills of this level.

It is even better if you can get your child to memorize the song. Many piano teachers do not require their students to memorize their music, but I believe memorizing recital songs makes them a better musician. Also, it helps them with their school academics. It increases their memory ability and their ability to focus and that translates to an easier time in their school work.

Don't just have them practice their song, but have them practice performing. This means have them play their recital song by memory for their friends, or at their school or at their church. Let them feel the experience of getting nervous before the actual recital. Teach them during these times and during lessons to play to the end no matter what happens. We never start over and we never give up no matter how bad a mistake might feel. We always finish because that's ultimately what piano is about. It's not about being perfect. It's about finishing and working hard and making beautiful music in the process.

Have your child be able to get dressed up for the occasion. Really make them feel like what they accomplished is a big deal...because it is! In their nice clothes with the audience on the couch watching, have them stand in front of the piano and say, "My name is (insert first and last name) and I will be playing (Insert name of song they are playing)."

Have them announce their song because it is a good skill to practice public speaking early on and it gives them more confidence. Then they should sit at the piano and begin to play. Remind them before the big day that they don't stop even if they make a mistake. Get to the end. We aim for perfection, but it's ok if there are mistakes. It's really about the people that love them celebrating their hard work.

Once their song is complete, have them stand up and bow for the people in the room (or on zoom) watching their performance.

Now is time to celebrate! Have some cookies and soda and have a party with the people you have over. Who doesn't want an excuse to get together with those we love! What better excuse than to celebrate the accomplishment of your child, and you, finishing a year of piano lessons!

If there's no family or friends to have over you can still make it special. Have your child get dressed up and do all the same performance items listed above. When they are done go out for ice cream. Let them know you are proud of them and celebrate their accomplishment of sticking with it and working hard!

This will give them the motivation to continue learning piano as well as give them the special memories they will cherish their whole life. These memories were made with YOU being their teacher. That is a priceless gift.

MOVING ON TO THE NEXT LEVEL

This is the last lesson of this book before moving on to the next level. Your child deserves a lot praise, that's quite an accomplishment!

Before starting the next book, it is very important that every concept taught in this book is understood by your child. If there is something your child still struggles with, take a few weeks and focus on that skill to help your child master it. Piano is like math. The skills build upon one another and if you move on without a strong foundation your child will quickly become frustrated and loose interest in the piano.

Finishing this book is the equivalent of finishing any of the 2nd lesson books paid teachers typically use. In the Faber piano adventure series and the Bastien piano basic method book your child has done the equivalent of finishing their level 1 book and your child should be ready to begin their level 2a book. I personally prefer the Faber series, but either are a good method book.

Don't feel like your child is too advanced for you to continue teaching your child. They are still at a beginning enough level that the parent is perfectly capable of teaching them and moving on to the next level of this book. Just make sure that they are having curved fingers on every note and their wrist is level with their hand not higher or lower than their hand. Those are the two biggest technique elements that an paid teacher would help correct at this stage.

There is not just a monetary advantage to continuing with this book to the next level and saving another years worth of tuition. There is a direct correlation in piano students success with how involved the parents are. Parents that sit in on the lesson and sit in on their child's practice time to make sure they are practicing correctly have children who are far more successful at the piano and learn at a faster rate.

You learning alongside your child in these first few levels is giving you an understanding of piano so that you can continue to help them as they move on to more advanced levels.

You can do it! Stick with teaching your child and give them a gift no teacher could ever give them... a memory and bond of parent and child learning a lifelong skill. If you feel the music is getting more challenging than the book can accommodate, try my online course. Still a fraction of the yearly cost of lessons, but you can hear each weeks lesson song played for you to make sure your child is playing it correctly and it is also filled with video lessons of the content to make understanding the material easier.

TEACHING THE PRACTICE SONG:

This song is in C position for both hands at the start of the song. Remind your child that each white note gets one finger. That means the E note is assigned to the 3rd finger for both hands. Whenever there is an E-Flat the 3rd finger will play it.

There is a hand shift in measure 10 for the right hand where it plays a treble G. It is not written into the music so your child needs to start looking for the change in the music itself to know to move hands.

The last step is to add pedal and dynamics to the piece after they have mastered all the rhythms and notes.

Don't forget the 8va at the very last measure where your child should be playing the C above treble C.

Daily Practice Log (4-6 days @ 15-20 minutes each day):

- ❇ *Flashcards for terms*
- ❇ *Flashcards for all notes (find the location on the piano)*
- ❇ *Practice song*
- ❇ *Corresponding Theory Chapter*
- ❇ *Hands together C & G & D & F Scale going up and down*
- ❇ *Flashcards all treble clef ledger lines combined*
- ❇ *Flashcard bass clef ledger line notes combined*
- ❇ *Major chords order C to B*

PRACTICE SONG lesson 4: Starry Night

Starry Night

Starry Night

Practice song answer for parents... Don't let your child see this answer at any time:

Other Resources From This Author:

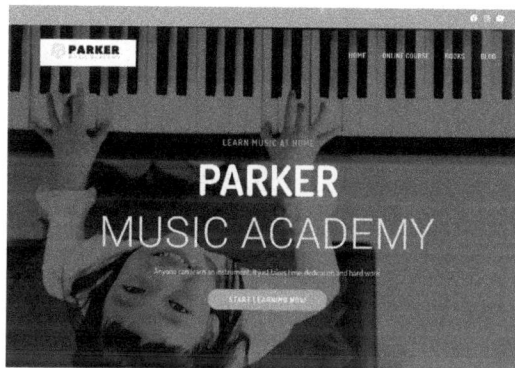

**Join the Parker Music Academy
Online Community**

Free resources, Online Course, Community
of like-minded parents and teachers and more.

parkermusicacademy.us

About The Author:

Stephanie Parker has played classical piano for over 35 years. She attended Florida State University College of Music with a concentration in piano. She has been teaching piano for over 20 years as well as been a homeschooling mom since 2006. Homeschooling her children has given her a unique skill set to learn how to teach effectively mainly age ranges with many differing abilities. It has also shown her parents are very capable of teaching their children many subjects with the proper help which is why she wants to create this book to help parents who want to give the gift of music to their child, but may not have the time or money to do so.

www.ingramcontent.com/pod-product-compliance
Lightning Source LLC
Chambersburg PA
CBHW081249040426
42452CB00015B/2757